Company's Coming ®

30-Minute Pantry
Recipes for What's on Hand

Jean Paré

www.companyscoming.com
visit our website

Front Cover

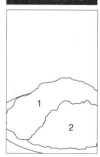

1. Creamy Mushroom
   Pork Chops, page 56
2. Couscous Primavera,
   page 131

Props: Mikasa

Back Cover

1. Fall Apple Salad,
   page 44
2. Cranberry-Crusted
   Salmon, page 91
3. Cranberry Coconut
   Brownies, page 137

Props: Sango

30-Minute Pantry

Copyright © Company's Coming Publishing Limited

All rights reserved worldwide. No part of this book may be reproduced, stored in a retrieval system or transmitted in any form by any means without written permission in advance from the publisher.

In the case of photocopying or other reprographic copying, a license may be purchased from the Canadian Copyright Licensing Agency (Access Copyright). Visit www.accesscopyright.ca or call toll free 1-800-893-5777. In the United States, please contact the Copyright Clearance Centre at www.copyright.com or call 978-646-8600.

Brief portions of this book may be reproduced for review purposes, provided credit is given to the source. Reviewers are invited to contact the publisher for additional information.

Fifth Printing March 2011

Library and Archives Canada Cataloguing in Publication

Paré, Jean, date
30-minute pantry : recipes for what's on hand / Jean Paré.
(Original series)
Includes index.
At head of title: Company's Coming.
ISBN 978-1-897477-29-8
1. Quick and easy cookery. I. Title.
II. Title: Thirty-minute pantry.
III. Series: Paré, Jean, date. Original series.
TX833.5.P374 2010   641.5'55   C2009-903051-9

Published by
Company's Coming Publishing Limited
2311 – 96 Street
Edmonton, Alberta, Canada T6N 1G3
Tel: 780-450-6223   Fax: 780-450-1857
www.companyscoming.com

Company's Coming is a registered trademark owned by Company's Coming Publishing Limited

We acknowledge the financial support of the Government of Canada through the Canada Book Fund for our publishing activities.

Printed in China

We gratefully acknowledge the following suppliers for their generous support of our Test and Photography Kitchens:

Broil King Barbecues
Corelle®
Hamilton Beach® Canada
Lagostina®
Proctor Silex® Canada
Tupperware®

Our special thanks to the following businesses for providing props for photography:

Stokes

Get more great recipes...FREE!

click

search

print

cook

From apple pie to zucchini bread, we've got you covered. Browse our free online recipes for Guaranteed Great!™ results.

You can also sign up to receive our **FREE online newsletter**. You'll receive exclusive offers, FREE recipes & cooking tips, new title previews, and much more...all delivered to your in-box.

So don't delay, visit our website today!

www.companyscoming.com
visit our ↟ website

Company's Coming Cookbooks

Quick & easy recipes; everyday ingredients!

Original Series

- Softcover, 160 pages
- Lay-flat plastic comb binding
- Full-colour photos
- Nutrition information

Original Series

- Softcover, 160 pages
- Lay-flat plastic comb binding
- Full-colour photos
- Nutrition information

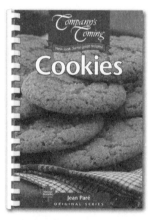

2-in-1 Cookbook Collection

- Softcover, 256 pages
- Lay-flat plastic coil binding
- Full-colour photos
- Nutrition information

Original Series

- Softcover, 160 pages
- Lay-flat plastic comb binding
- Full-colour photos
- Updated format

For a complete listing of our cookbooks, visit our website:
www.companyscoming.com

Table of Contents

Breakfast

Sandwiches
& Wraps

Soups & Salads

Entrees

Side Dishes

Desserts

Snacks

The Company's Coming Story

Jean Paré (pronounced "jeen PAIR-ee") grew up understanding that the combination of family, friends and home cooking is the best recipe for a good life. From her mother, she learned to appreciate good cooking, while her father praised even her earliest attempts in the kitchen. When Jean left home, she took with her a love of cooking, many family recipes and an intriguing desire to read cookbooks as if they were novels!

"Never share a recipe you wouldn't use yourself."

When her four children had all reached school age, Jean volunteered to cater the 50th anniversary celebration of the Vermilion School of Agriculture, now Lakeland College, in Alberta, Canada. Working out of her home, Jean prepared a dinner for more than 1,000 people, launching a flourishing catering operation that continued for over 18 years. During that time, she had countless opportunities to test new ideas with immediate feedback—resulting in empty plates and contented customers! Whether preparing cocktail sandwiches for a house party or serving a hot meal for 1,500 people, Jean Paré earned a reputation for great food, courteous service and reasonable prices.

As requests for her recipes increased, Jean was often asked the question, "Why don't you write a cookbook?" Jean responded by teaming up with her son, Grant Lovig, in the fall of 1980 to form Company's Coming Publishing Limited. The publication of *150 Delicious Squares* on April 14, 1981 marked the debut of what would soon become one of the world's most popular cookbook series.

The company has grown since those early days when Jean worked from a spare bedroom in her home. Today, she continues to write recipes while working closely with the staff of the Recipe Factory, as the Company's Coming test kitchen is affectionately known.

There she fills the role of mentor, assisting with the development of recipes people most want to use for everyday cooking and easy entertaining. Every Company's Coming recipe is *kitchen-tested* before it is approved for publication.

Jean's daughter, Gail Lovig, is responsible for marketing and distribution, leading a team that includes sales personnel located in major cities across Canada. Company's Coming cookbooks are distributed in Canada, the United States, Australia and other world markets. Bestsellers many times over in English, Company's Coming cookbooks have also been published in French and Spanish.

Familiar and trusted in home kitchens around the world, Company's Coming cookbooks are offered in a variety of formats. Highly regarded as kitchen workbooks, the softcover Original Series, with its lay-flat plastic comb binding, is still a favourite among readers.

Jean Paré's approach to cooking has always called for *quick and easy recipes* using *everyday ingredients*. That view has served her well. The recipient of many awards, including the Queen Elizabeth Golden Jubilee Medal, Jean was appointed Member of the Order of Canada, her country's highest lifetime achievement honour.

Jean continues to gain new supporters by adhering to what she calls The Golden Rule of Cooking: *Never share a recipe you wouldn't use yourself.* It's an approach that has worked—*millions of times over!*

Foreword

What's the point of having a pantry full of food if you never have the time to cook it, and you're not even sure what to do with it?

30-Minute Pantry is packed with tips on shopping, storing and prepping today's pantry so you'll be able to get great meals on the table in less than half an hour. Cooking this way will save you money and help you avoid heading to fast-food outlets as a mealtime solution.

To get meals to the table in under 30 minutes while using only ingredients on hand, you'll have to use basic foods in unique and delicious ways. We've created a pantry list that features everyday ingredients that most people will have on hand, and we've worked hard to develop recipes that use grilling, stovetop and microwave methods to save you time. We've also used basic pantry staples like pasta sauces or salsa to quickly give complex flavour in the minimum time.

From Breakfast Parfaits to Black Bean Burritos, and Chocolate Crunch Clusters to Chili Pork Chops, the recipes in this book cover a wide range of foods and offer plenty of options for meal ideas that also make the most of your pantry.

By keeping your pantry stocked with the items recommended on our list, you can make any of these recipes quickly and easily.

Explore the recipes in this book and you'll find something for every occasion and all taste buds. From breakfasts to desserts and everything in between, whether you need to feed just yourself, or there's a crowd arriving unexpectedly, you'll rise to the occasion. With *30-Minute Pantry* you'll have delicious meals ready in a hurry from ingredients you already have.

Jean Paré

Nutrition Information Guidelines

Each recipe is analyzed using the most current version of the Canadian Nutrient File from Health Canada, which is based on the United States Department of Agriculture (USDA) Nutrient Database.

- If more than one ingredient is listed (such as "butter or hard margarine"), or if a range is given (1 – 2 tsp., 5 – 10 mL), only the first ingredient or first amount is analyzed.

- For meat, poultry and fish, the serving size per person is based on the recommended 4 oz. (113 g) uncooked weight (without bone), which is 2 – 3 oz. (57 – 85 g) cooked weight (without bone)—approximately the size of a deck of playing cards.

- Milk used is 1% M.F. (milk fat), unless otherwise stated.

- Cooking oil used is canola oil, unless otherwise stated.

- Ingredients indicating "sprinkle," "optional," or "for garnish" are not included in the nutrition information.

- The fat in recipes and combination foods can vary greatly depending on the sources and types of fats used in each specific ingredient. For these reasons, the amount of saturated, monounsaturated and polyunsaturated fats may not add up to the total fat content.

Vera C. Mazurak, Ph.D.
Nutritionist

The Evolution of the Pantry: Tradition vs. Modern Convenience

Traditionally, our grandparents and great-grandparents stocked their pantries based on very simple principles. They needed food that would last them through frozen winters and changing seasons. Food availability was limited by shelf life and storage options, so if no food was put away, there really wasn't anything to eat. Modern conveniences like grocery stores and 24-hour marts have all but eliminated the necessity of the pantry. But with the modern dilemma of never having enough time but still needing to eat well, a well-stocked pantry is your greatest defence against poor food choices and too much take-out.

With advances in technology, such as energy-efficient appliances and freshness-sealing packaging, you can keep a greater variety of foods on hand. Now, without emergency trips to the store, you can get the food on the table—fast.

We've poked through our own cupboards, freezers and fridges and discovered some great items that update the idea of cooking with staples. Today we can rely on having balsamic vinegar in the cupboard and fresh vegetables in the fridge.

Ease and Convenience

With your food storage areas (pantry, freezer, fridge) stocked with some simple ingredients (see our Pantry List, page 11) and our recipes, you can guarantee that whether it's just you, a full table or some unexpected guests, you'll have a meal ready in 30 minutes or less.

We've even added some super-quick recipes, with only five or six ingredients, that will go from pantry to table in less than 15 minutes.

Flexibility and Versatility

The recipes in this book take the items in your pantry to breakfast, lunch, dinner and all the snacks and occasions in between. Think peanut butter is just for PBJ sandwiches? We'll show you how to use it in Thai Tofu Steaks, Chocolate Crunch Clusters, a Chicken Satay Stir-Fry and several other dishes. Or use that jar of salsa for more than dipping chips by adding it to 12 recipes with southwestern flair!

Most of the recipes in this book are for four people. Feeding more or less than that? We've got recipes for that too, but remember that most recipes can be easily doubled. To get the best results when adjusting for yield, test seasoning at one and a half times the original volume and then add more to taste. Oils for cooking (in a frying pan or saucepan, for instance) might not need to be doubled. Start with the original amount and add extra as necessary.

If you've just made too much—great! Packed up into individual servings, leftovers make fantastic ready-to-go meals for later in the week.

Shopping

Stocking a pantry for quick meal-making takes just a little planning. We know you're busy, but a little extra time up front will translate to much more time saved later. Check out the Pantry List on page 11 and you'll probably notice that you have most of the items already. If there's something you don't have, is it because you don't like it? Or because you didn't know it could be versatile enough to be worth having around?

Keep a list of items you notice getting low throughout the week. Then sit down and plan your meals from this book for the upcoming week. Check what you need against what you have and make your list, including any staples that are running low.

You'll notice that with a carefully planned list it's easier to stick to the perimeter of the grocery store, where healthier, less-processed items are found, with fewer trips into the centre aisles. Your grocery trips become more focused, further apart and quicker, and you're more likely to bring home healthier foods.

Storage

We don't all have our dream kitchen and storage can be at a premium, but that doesn't mean you have to give up on being well stocked. The updated pantry includes not only a cupboard where dry and canned goods are stored, but also your refrigerator for storing fresh produce, dairy and tofu, as well as your freezer, for stocking up on frozen meats, vegetables and fruits.

Notice you don't go through a lot of something? Try buying in smaller quantities from the bulk section and storing in airtight containers. Often items like roasted nuts, dried fruit and baking staples are cheaper when purchased in bulk, and you can buy just the amount that you can store conveniently.

Remember that dried spices don't last forever! We recommend buying small quantities from the bulk section and storing them in labelled, airtight containers.

9

Once you've brought home your shopping for the week, spend a little time pre-prepping and storing it. Make a list of what items will need to be defrosted when, and post it where you'll see it regularly. Separate large quantities into individual recipe-size amounts and freeze or refrigerate for quick grabbing later. Things like bacon slices can be frozen in a single layer on a cookie sheet prior to repacking. That way, when you only need four slices, you don't have to defrost a whole package. Bulk purchases of ground meats or chicken pieces can be packed up in 1 pound (454 g) packages. Large fruits, like melons or fresh pineapple, can be peeled and chopped and stored in airtight containers in the fridge so you'll have easy and healthy snacks on hand! Similarly, you can store snack-friendly vegetables like celery, baby carrots and sugar snap peas in individual serving-sized packages.

Lastly, if you find yourself with leftover canned beans or corn, these can become great additions to salads, soups and stews, or try them in one of our other recipes!

Time-Saving Tips

When it comes to cooking time, here's how to make sure the food is ready in under 30 minutes:

- **Save cooking time by starting with hot tap water.** When every second counts, don't waste time waiting for the pot to boil!

- **Start from thawed.** Because in most recipes, defrosting is not included in the 30-minute time limit, we suggest you defrost meat, seafood and vegetables or fruits by placing them in the fridge the morning or evening before you need them. You can also rinse them under cool or lukewarm water to thaw them quickly. Microwaves have defrost cycles, but using the microwave can compromise quality and add preparation time.

- **Plan ahead for softened or room-temperature items.** To reduce prep time, pull items like cream cheese, butter or eggs from the fridge as soon as you get in the door after work. By the time you've gotten the kids into their homework, put away your work gear and assembled your other ingredients, your items will likely have had time to come to room temperature.

- **Pre-cook where possible.** Once you've planned and shopped, prepping can include cooking. Just store pre-cooked items like crisped and crumbled bacon or hard-cooked eggs in airtight, refrigerated containers until needed. Grains and rice are also ideal candidates for pre-cooking. When you're ready for them, just reheat and serve.

Pantry List

Below is our ultimate pantry list. Once you have all of these items, you're ready to make anything in this book!

Fresh Produce

Fruit
apples, bananas, lemons, limes, and oranges

Vegetables
bell peppers, carrots, celery, English cucumber, garlic, green onion, lettuce (iceberg and romaine), onions, potatoes, tomatoes, and white mushrooms

Other
medium tofu

Eggs & Dairy

Cheeses
Cheddar (medium), cream cheese (block, plain), feta, Mexican cheese blend (grated), and Parmesan (grated)

Yogurt
fruit and plain

Other
butter, eggs, milk, and sour cream

Breads & Deli

Bread
brown bread (sliced), flour tortillas (plain, 9 inch, 22 cm), bread crumbs (fine, dry), and white bread (sliced)

Deli Meats
ham and turkey

Frozen

Fish & Seafood
fish fillets (haddock, salmon, and sole), shrimp (uncooked medium, peeled and deveined)

Fruit
mango and mixed berries

Meats
bacon slices, beef steak (top sirloin), breakfast sausage, chicken breast (boneless, skinless), chicken thighs (boneless, skinless), ground chicken, ground turkey, lean ground beef, pork chops (fast-fry), and pork tenderloin

Vegetables
mixed vegetables (with peas, corn, green beans and carrot), Oriental mixed vegetables, and peas

Other
orange juice (concentrated)

Canned/Bottled

Bottled
liquid honey, maple syrup, and salad dressings (Caesar, Italian, and ranch)

Canned
baked beans in tomato sauce, beef broth (prepared), black beans, chickpeas (garbanzo beans), chicken broth (prepared), condensed cream of mushroom soup, kernel corn, lentils, light flaked tuna (in water), pear halves, peaches (sliced in juice/syrup), pineapple tidbits, pink salmon, tomato paste, tomato sauce, and tomatoes (diced)

Jarred
applesauce (unsweetened), dill pickles, jam (apricot and raspberry), pasta sauce (alfredo and tomato), peanut butter (smooth), and roasted red peppers

Dried

Dried Fruit
apricots, cranberries, and raisins

Pasta
egg noodles (medium), elbow macaroni, fusilli, and spaghetti

Sugar
brown and granulated

Other
almonds (sliced), baking powder, baking soda, biscuit mix, chocolate chips, cocoa powder, coconut (medium unsweetened), cornstarch, couscous (plain), flour (all-purpose), granola, rice (white), rolled oats (quick-cooking), and sunflower seeds.

Herbs, Seasonings & Condiments

Condiments
barbecue sauce, basil pesto, Dijon mustard, ketchup, mayonnaise, salsa, sambal oelek (chili paste), soy sauce, sweet chili sauce, and Worcestershire sauce

Dried Herbs & Spices
allspice (ground), basil, cayenne pepper, chili powder, cinnamon (ground), crushed chillies, cumin (ground), curry powder, dillweed, garlic powder, ginger (ground), Montreal steak spice, oregano, pepper, salt, seasoned salt, and thyme

Oils
cooking oil, cooking spray, olive oil, and sesame oil

Vinegars
balsamic and white

Other
vanilla extract

Breakfast Parfaits

Sunny-coloured fruit is tossed in a tangy dressing and layered with granola and yogurt. Dig deep and get a bit of each in every bite.

Liquid honey	2 tbsp.	30 mL
Lemon juice	1 tsp.	5 mL
Ground cinnamon	1/8 tsp.	0.5 mL
Can of sliced peaches in juice, drained, chopped	14 oz.	398 mL
Large banana, sliced	1	1
Mixed berry yogurt	1/2 cup	125 mL
Granola	1/2 cup	125 mL

Combine first 3 ingredients in medium bowl.

Add peaches and banana. Stir until coated. Spoon into 2 dessert bowls.

Layer yogurt and granola, in order given, over peach mixture. Makes 2 parfaits.

1 parfait: 412 Calories; 3.5 g Total Fat (0.1 g Mono, 0.1 g Poly, 0.3 g Sat); 5 mg Cholesterol; 94 g Carbohydrate; 8 g Fibre; 6 g Protein; 55 mg Sodium

Banana Maple French Toast

Who doesn't have time for a quick, sweet treat? Try this golden French toast with maple-fried bananas next time you're craving a sweet breakfast.

FRENCH TOAST		
Butter	1 tbsp.	15 mL
Large eggs	2	2
Milk	1/2 cup	125 mL
Granulated sugar	2 tsp.	10 mL
Salt, sprinkle		
White (or whole-wheat) bread slices	4	4
BANANA TOPPING		
Butter	1 tbsp.	15 mL
Sliced banana (1/2 inch, 12 mm, slices)	2 cups	500 mL
Maple syrup	1/4 cup	60 mL

French Toast: Melt butter in large frying pan on medium.

Meanwhile, whisk next 4 ingredients in small shallow bowl.

Dip bread slices into egg mixture. Turn to coat both sides. Add to pan. Pour any remaining egg mixture over top. Cook for about 2 minutes per side until browned. Transfer to 4 serving plates.

Banana Topping: Melt butter in medium frying pan on medium. Add banana. Heat and stir for 1 minute.

Add syrup. Stir. Spoon banana topping over toast. Serves 4.

1 serving: 292 Calories; 9.4 g Total Fat (1.8 g Mono, 0.6 g Poly, 4.8 g Sat); 124 mg Cholesterol; 47 g Carbohydrate; 3 g Fibre; 7 g Protein; 262 mg Sodium

Peachy Pear Crepes

Plenty of fruit in a delicate and easy crepe—just peachy! A sweetened yogurt sauce makes a deliciously creamy topping.

Large eggs	2	2
All-purpose flour	1/2 cup	125 mL
Milk	1/2 cup	125 mL
Water	1 tbsp.	15 mL
Cooking oil	1 1/2 tsp.	7 mL
Salt	1/8 tsp.	0.5 mL
Cooking oil	1 tsp.	5 mL
Can of pear halves in juice, drained, sliced	14 oz.	398 mL
Can of sliced peaches in juice, drained	14 oz.	398 mL
Peach yogurt	1/2 cup	125 mL
Peach yogurt	1/4 cup	60 mL

Whisk first 6 ingredients in medium bowl until smooth.

Heat 1/4 tsp. (1 mL) cooking oil in medium non-stick frying pan on medium. Pour about 1/3 cup (75 mL) batter into pan. Immediately tilt and swirl pan to ensure bottom is covered. Cook for about 1 minute until top is set. Turn. Cook for about 1 minute until brown spots appear on bottom. Transfer to plate. Cover to keep warm. Repeat with remaining batter, adding and heating cooking oil between batches to prevent sticking.

Combine next 3 ingredients in small bowl. Place crepes on 4 serving plates. Spoon pear mixture across centre of each crepe. Roll up to enclose filling.

Drizzle with second amount of yogurt. Makes 4 crepes.

1 crepe: 309 Calories; 6.1 g Total Fat (1.8 g Mono, 0.9 g Poly, 1.4 g Sat); 111 mg Cholesterol; 59 g Carbohydrate; 5 g Fibre; 7 g Protein; 149 mg Sodium

Paré Pointer

Polite chickens say "eggs-cuse me."

Big Breakfast Frittata

Start your big day with a big breakfast frittata chock full of ham, mushrooms, peppers and cheese.

Cooking oil	1 tsp.	5 mL
Chopped deli ham	1 cup	250 mL
Sliced fresh white mushrooms	1 cup	250 mL
Chopped red pepper	1/2 cup	125 mL
Chopped green onion	1/4 cup	60 mL
Large eggs	8	8
Dried oregano	1/2 tsp.	2 mL
Salt, just a pinch		
Pepper, just a pinch		
Grated Cheddar cheese	1/2 cup	125 mL
Chopped tomato	1/2 cup	125 mL
Chopped green onion	1 tbsp.	15 mL

Heat cooking oil in large non-stick frying pan on medium. Add next 4 ingredients. Cook for about 5 minutes, stirring occasionally, until red pepper is softened.

Whisk next 4 ingredients in medium bowl. Pour over ham mixture. Reduce heat to medium-low. Cook, covered, for about 10 minutes until bottom is golden and top is set. Remove from heat.

Sprinkle with cheese. Let stand for about 1 minute until cheese is melted.

Sprinkle with tomato and second amount of green onion. Cuts into 4 wedges.

1 wedge: 253 Calories; 15.4 g Total Fat (2.0 g Mono, 0.5 g Poly, 6.1 g Sat); 461 mg Cholesterol; 6 g Carbohydrate; 1 g Fibre; 23 g Protein; 701 mg Sodium

Pictured at right.

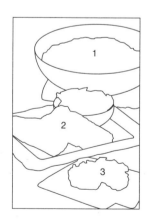

1. Big Breakfast Frittata, above
2. Stuffed French Toast, page 21
3. Country Biscuits with Cranberry Orange Butter, page 26

Props: Bella Cucina

Denver Scramble

A ham-and-egg classic gets a lift from cheese, peppers and onions.
Rustle up the family and dig in.

Butter	1 tbsp.	15 mL
Chopped deli ham	3/4 cup	175 mL
Chopped green pepper	1/4 cup	60 mL
Chopped onion	1/4 cup	60 mL
Large eggs	8	8
Water	1/4 cup	60 mL
Seasoned salt	1/4 tsp.	1 mL
Pepper	1/8 tsp.	0.5 mL
Grated Cheddar cheese	3/4 cup	175 mL

Melt butter in large frying pan on medium. Add next 3 ingredients. Cook for about 5 minutes, stirring often, until onion is softened.

Whisk next 4 ingredients in small bowl. Pour over ham mixture. Stir slowly and constantly with spatula, scraping sides and bottom of pan until eggs are set and liquid is evaporated.

Add cheese. Heat and stir for about 2 minutes until cheese is melted. Serve immediately. Makes about 3 1/2 cups (875 mL).

1/2 cup (125 mL): 161 Calories; 11.0 g Total Fat (1.6 g Mono, 0.2 g Poly, 5.3 g Sat); 270 mg Cholesterol; 3 g Carbohydrate; trace Fibre; 13 g Protein; 431 mg Sodium

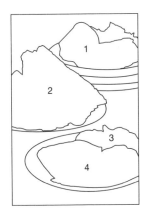

1. Greek Chicken Wraps, page 31
2. Rainbow Deli Sandwich, page 27
3. Papas Bravas, page 129
4. Ham and Veggie Burritos, page 32

Props: Studio Nova

Mango Pancakes

Don't let the contents of your pantry fool you—exotic breakfasts are at your fingertips. These fluffy pancakes have lots of mango pieces and just the right amount of ginger spice. Try them with maple syrup.

All-purpose flour	1 cup	250 mL
Granulated sugar	1 tbsp.	15 mL
Baking powder	1 tsp.	5 mL
Ground ginger	3/4 tsp.	4 mL
Baking soda	1/2 tsp.	2 mL
Salt	1/4 tsp.	1 mL
Large egg	1	1
Frozen mango pieces, thawed	1 1/2 cups	375 mL
Milk	1/4 cup	60 mL
Cooking oil	2 tbsp.	30 mL
Lime juice	1 tbsp.	15 mL
Finely chopped frozen mango pieces, thawed	1/2 cup	125 mL

Preheat griddle to medium-high (see Note). Combine first 6 ingredients in large bowl. Make a well in centre.

Process next 5 ingredients in blender until smooth. Add to well.

Add second amount of mango. Stir until just combined. Batter will be lumpy. Spray griddle with cooking spray. Pour batter onto griddle, using 1/3 cup (75 mL) for each pancake. Cook for about 2 minutes until bubbles form on top and edges appear dry. Turn pancake over. Cook for about 2 minutes until bottom is golden. Transfer to plate. Cover to keep warm. Repeat with remaining batter, spraying griddle with more cooking spray if necessary to prevent sticking. Makes about 6 pancakes.

1 pancake: 161 Calories; 5.7 g Total Fat (2.8 g Mono, 1.4 g Poly, 0.7 g Sat); 36 mg Cholesterol; 25 g Carbohydrate; 1 g Fibre; 4 g Protein; 311 mg Sodium

Note: If you don't have an electric griddle, use a large frying pan. Replace cooking spray with 1 tsp. (5 mL) cooking oil and heat on medium. Heat more cooking oil with each batch if necessary to prevent sticking.

Stuffed French Toast

Make your Sunday brunch stand out from the crowd with a cream cheese and berry centre in your French toast.

Block cream cheese, softened	1/2 cup	125 mL
Granulated sugar	2 tbsp.	30 mL
Frozen mixed berries, thawed and drained, larger pieces chopped	1/2 cup	125 mL
Whole-wheat (or white) bread slices	8	8
Cooking oil	1 tbsp.	15 mL
Large eggs	2	2
Milk	1 cup	250 mL
Vanilla extract	1 tsp.	5 mL
Ground cinnamon, just a pinch (optional)		
Maple syrup (optional)	1/4 cup	60 mL

Beat cream cheese and sugar in medium bowl for about 3 minutes until sugar is dissolved and mixture is smooth.

Add berries. Stir. Spread over 4 bread slices. Cover with remaining bread slices. Press down lightly.

Heat cooking oil in large frying pan on medium.

Meanwhile, whisk next 4 ingredients in medium shallow bowl. Dip sandwiches into egg mixture. Turn to coat both sides. Add to pan. Cook for about 4 minutes per side until golden brown. Transfer to serving plates.

Drizzle with syrup. Serves 4.

1 serving: 366 Calories; 18.7 g Total Fat (3.2 g Mono, 1.6 g Poly, 8.9 g Sat); 141 mg Cholesterol; 39 g Carbohydrate; 4 g Fibre; 13 g Protein; 460 mg Sodium

Pictured on page 17.

Paré Pointer

If we breathe oxygen during the day, do we breathe night-rogen at night?

Fruit Salad Sipsters

This lovely smoothie is a sip-able fruit salad in a glass.

Milk	1 cup	250 mL
Mixed berry yogurt	1/2 cup	125 mL
Canned sliced peaches, drained	1/3 cup	75 mL
Frozen mixed berries	1/3 cup	75 mL
Liquid honey	2 tbsp.	30 mL
Ice cubes	4	4
Frozen overripe medium banana, cut up (see Note)	1	1

Process all 7 ingredients in blender until smooth. Pour into glasses. Makes about 3 2/3 cups (900 mL).

1 cup (250 mL): 73 Calories; 0.5 g Total Fat (0.1 g Mono, trace Poly, 0.3 g Sat); 3 mg Cholesterol; 16 g Carbohydrate; 1 g Fibre; 2 g Protein; 27 mg Sodium

Note: To use up bananas that are too ripe to enjoy fresh, peel and cut them into 2 inch (5 cm) chunks and freeze them on a baking sheet. Once frozen, transfer them to a resealable freezer bag to use in any blended drink you like. Ripe bananas have great flavour for beverages.

Sausage Biscuits

If there are any leftovers, keep them in the refrigerator for breakfasts on the go or to accompany a soup lunch.

Cooking oil	1 tsp.	5 mL
Breakfast sausage, casing removed	1/2 lb.	225 g
Finely chopped onion	1/2 cup	125 mL
Pepper	1/4 tsp.	1 mL
Biscuit mix	2 cups	500 mL
Grated Cheddar cheese	1 cup	250 mL
Milk	1/2 cup	125 mL
Milk	1 tbsp.	15 mL

(continued on next page)

Preheat oven to 450°F (230°C). Heat cooking oil in large frying pan on medium-high. Add next 3 ingredients. Scramble-fry for about 5 minutes until sausage is browned. Drain.

Combine biscuit mix and cheese in medium bowl. Make a well in centre. Add first amount of milk and sausage mixture. Stir until just moistened. Turn out onto lightly floured surface. Knead 8 times. Roll or pat out to 8 inch (20 cm) square. Cut into 2 inch (5 cm) squares. Arrange on greased baking sheet with sides.

Brush with second amount of milk. Bake for about 10 minutes until wooden pick inserted in centre of biscuit comes out clean. Makes 16 biscuits.

1 biscuit: 120 Calories; 6.5 g Total Fat (1.7 g Mono, 0.4 g Poly, 2.6 g Sat); 14 mg Cholesterol; 11 g Carbohydrate; trace Fibre; 5 g Protein; 303 mg Sodium

Aloha Oatmeal

Need a holiday but just can't get one? Make your breakfast your vacation with all the aloha flavour of pineapple juice-sweetened oatmeal studded with pineapple bits, banana and coconut.

Water	1 1/4 cups	300 mL
Reserved pineapple juice	3/4 cup	175 mL
Salt	1/8 tsp.	0.5 mL
Can of pineapple tidbits, drained and juice reserved	14 oz.	398 mL
Quick-cooking rolled oats	1 cup	250 mL
Medium unsweetened coconut	1/3 cup	75 mL
Diced banana	3/4 cup	175 mL
Vanilla extract	1/2 tsp.	2 mL

Combine first 3 ingredients in medium saucepan. Bring to a boil. Reduce heat to medium-low.

Add next 3 ingredients. Stir. Cook, uncovered, for about 5 minutes, stirring often, until thickened.

Add banana and vanilla. Stir. Makes about 3 1/2 cups (875 mL).

1/2 cup (125 mL): 134 Calories; 3.3 g Total Fat (0.1 g Mono, 0.1 g Poly, 2.0 g Sat); 0 mg Cholesterol; 25 g Carbohydrate; 3 g Fibre; 2 g Protein; 44 mg Sodium

Huevos Rancheros

Got a craving for warmth on a cold morning? Turn up the heat on this eggy breakfast by using your preference of salsa.

Olive (or cooking) oil	1 tbsp.	15 mL
Thinly sliced onion	1/4 cup	60 mL
Thinly sliced yellow pepper	1/4 cup	60 mL
Garlic clove, minced	1	1
(or 1/4 tsp., 1 mL, powder)		
Ground cumin	1/4 tsp.	1 mL
Cayenne pepper	1/8 tsp.	0.5 mL
Salsa	1 1/2 cups	375 mL
Water	1/4 cup	60 mL
Large eggs	8	8
Grated medium Cheddar cheese	1/4 cup	60 mL
Flour tortillas (9 inch, 22 cm, diameter), quartered	4	4
Cooking spray		

Preheat broiler. Heat olive oil in large frying pan on medium. Add next 5 ingredients. Cook for about 5 minutes, stirring often, until onion is softened.

Add salsa and water. Stir.

Reduce heat to medium-low. Break eggs, 1 at a time, into shallow dish. Slip each egg into salsa mixture in single layer around pan. Cook, covered, for 10 to 12 minutes until egg white is set and yolk reaches desired doneness. Spoon salsa mixture, with eggs on top, onto 4 serving plates. Sprinkle with cheese.

Meanwhile, arrange tortillas on greased baking sheet with sides. Spray with cooking spray. Broil for about 30 seconds per side until lightly browned. Arrange around salsa mixture. Serves 4.

1 serving: 368 Calories; 19.2 g Total Fat (3.2 g Mono, 0.6 g Poly, 6.0 g Sat); 437 mg Cholesterol; 31 g Carbohydrate; trace Fibre; 17 g Protein; 830 mg Sodium

Carrot Tops

These large cookies are reminiscent of carrot cake-flavoured muffin tops, but you don't have to be a redhead to enjoy them!

All-purpose flour	3/4 cup	175 mL
Brown sugar, packed	1/3 cup	75 mL
Quick-cooking rolled oats	1/4 cup	60 mL
Baking powder	1/2 tsp.	2 mL
Baking soda	1/4 tsp.	1 mL
Ground cinnamon	1/4 tsp.	1 mL
Salt	1/4 tsp.	1 mL
Ground allspice	1/8 tsp.	0.5 mL
Large egg, fork-beaten	1	1
Sour cream	1/3 cup	75 mL
Cooking oil	3 tbsp.	50 mL
Vanilla extract	1/4 tsp.	1 mL
Grated carrot	3/4 cup	175 mL
Sliced almonds	2 tbsp.	30 mL

Preheat oven to 375°F (190°C). Combine first 8 ingredients in large bowl. Make a well in centre.

Combine next 4 ingredients in medium bowl. Add to well.

Add carrot and almonds. Stir until just moistened. Drop, using 1/4 cup (60 mL) for each, about 2 inches (5 cm) apart on greased cookie sheet. Bake for about 12 minutes until wooden pick inserted in centre of cookie comes out clean. Let stand on cookie sheet for 5 minutes before removing to wire rack to cool slightly. Makes about 6 cookies.

1 cookie: 229 Calories; 11.4 g Total Fat (4.7 g Mono, 2.3 g Poly, 2.4 g Sat); 45 mg Cholesterol; 28 g Carbohydrate; 1 g Fibre; 4 g Protein; 225 mg Sodium

Paré Pointer

He is such an egotist—always me-deep in conversation.

Country Biscuits

Mix the Cranberry Orange Butter while the biscuits are baking and it'll be ready to spread on hot biscuits right out of the oven.

CHEESE BISCUITS

All-purpose flour	2 cups	500 mL
Baking powder	1 tbsp.	15 mL
Salt	1 tsp.	5 mL
Milk	1 cup	250 mL
Mayonnaise	1/3 cup	75 mL
Grated Cheddar cheese	3/4 cup	175 mL

CRANBERRY ORANGE BUTTER

Butter, softened	1/4 cup	60 mL
Finely chopped dried cranberries	1 1/2 tbsp.	25 mL
Liquid honey	2 tsp.	10 mL
Grated orange zest	1/2 tsp.	2 mL

Cheese Biscuits: Preheat oven to 400°F (205°C). Combine first 3 ingredients in large bowl. Make a well in centre.

Combine milk and mayonnaise in small bowl. Add to well. Add cheese. Stir until just moistened. Fill 12 greased muffin cups. Bake for about 15 minutes until wooden pick inserted in centre of biscuit comes out clean. Let stand in pan for 5 minutes. Remove to serving plate.

Cranberry Orange Butter: Meanwhile, combine all 4 ingredients in small bowl. Makes about 1/3 cup (75 mL). Serve with Cheese Biscuits. Makes 12 biscuits.

1 biscuit with 1 tsp. (5 mL) Cranberry Orange Butter: 192 Calories; 11.2 g Total Fat (1.7 g Mono, 0.2 g Poly, 4.7 g Sat); 21 mg Cholesterol; 18 g Carbohydrate; trace Fibre; 5 g Protein; 446 mg Sodium

Pictured on page 17.

Rainbow Deli Sandwiches

Silky cream cheese and a rainbow of crunchy fresh vegetables turn a regular ham sandwich into a treat.

Block cream cheese, softened	4 oz.	125 g
Italian dressing	2 tbsp.	30 mL
Dried oregano	1/4 tsp.	1 mL
Whole-wheat bread slices	4	4
Grated carrot, blotted dry	1/2 cup	125 mL
Deli ham slices	8	8
Thin English cucumber slices (with peel)	12	12
Thin tomato slices	12	12
Thin yellow pepper rings	8	8
Romaine lettuce mix	1 cup	250 mL
Whole-wheat bread slices	4	4

Stir first 3 ingredients in small bowl until smooth.

Spread over first 4 bread slices. Scatter carrot over top.

Layer next 5 ingredients, in order given, over carrot.

Cover with remaining bread slices. Makes 4 sandwiches.

1 sandwich: 309 Calories; 14.5 g Total Fat (1.0 g Mono, 0.7 g Poly, 7.4 g Sat); 48 mg Cholesterol; 32 g Carbohydrate; 5 g Fibre; 16 g Protein; 1100 mg Sodium

Pictured on page 18.

BBQ Turkey Melts

Put a tasty spin on tired turkey sammies with some barbecue sauce and melted cheese.

Barbecue sauce	2 tbsp.	30 mL
Mayonnaise	2 tbsp.	30 mL
Whole-wheat bread slices, toasted	4	4
Deli turkey breast slices, halved	8	8
Medium tomatoes, sliced	2	2
Cheddar cheese slices	4	4

Preheat broiler. Combine barbecue sauce and mayonnaise in small cup.

Arrange toast slices on baking sheet with sides. Spread barbecue sauce mixture over top.

Layer remaining 3 ingredients, in order given, over barbecue sauce mixture. Broil on centre rack in oven for about 5 minutes until cheese is melted. Makes 4 melts.

1 melt: 300 Calories; 17.2 g Total Fat (3.4 g Mono, 0.7 g Poly, 7.2 g Sat); 50 mg Cholesterol; 20 g Carbohydrate; 3 g Fibre; 18 g Protein; 854 mg Sodium

PB and Pickle Triangles

No, we're not pulling your leg, but this sandwich will tickle your taste buds in the most delightful way. If you're still not willing, try substituting banana for the pickles.

Smooth peanut butter	1/4 cup	60 mL
Whole-wheat (or white) bread slices, toasted	4	4
Medium dill pickles, thinly sliced lengthwise	2	2

Spread peanut butter over toast slices.

Arrange pickles over peanut butter on 2 toast slices. Cover with remaining toast slices. Cut each sandwich diagonally into quarters. Makes 8 triangles.

1 triangle: 85 Calories; 4.9 g Total Fat (0.2 g Mono, 0.2 g Poly, 1.0 g Sat); 0 mg Cholesterol; 9 g Carbohydrate; 2 g Fibre; 3 g Protein; 320 mg Sodium

Cheesy Pepper Beef Sandwiches

Who needs to go out for cheese steaks when you've got everything you need at home to make these juicy and delectable sandwiches?

Cooking oil	1 tsp.	5 mL
Dried basil	1/8 tsp.	0.5 mL
Dried oregano	1/8 tsp.	0.5 mL
Dried thyme	1/8 tsp.	0.5 mL
Salt	1/8 tsp.	0.5 mL
Pepper, sprinkle		
Beef top sirloin steak	1/2 lb.	225 g
Cream cheese, softened	4 oz.	125 g
Roasted red peppers, chopped	1/4 cup	60 mL
Cayenne pepper, sprinkle		
White bread slices, toasted	8	8
Cooking oil	1/2 tsp.	2 mL
Sliced onion	1/2 cup	125 mL

Combine first 6 ingredients in medium bowl.

Cut steak crosswise into 1/4 inch (6 mm) slices. Cut slices lengthwise into thin strips. Add to cooking oil mixture. Stir.

Combine next 3 ingredients in small bowl. Spread over toast slices.

Heat second amount of cooking oil in large frying pan or wok on medium-high until very hot. Add onion. Stir-fry for about 3 minutes until starting to brown. Add beef mixture. Stir-fry for about 3 minutes until beef reaches desired doneness. Spoon over cream cheese mixture on 4 toast slices. Cover with remaining toast slices. Makes 4 sandwiches.

1 sandwich: 354 Calories; 16.9 g Total Fat (3.0 g Mono, 1.3 g Poly, 8.7 g Sat); 59 mg Cholesterol; 30 g Carbohydrate; 1 g Fibre; 19 g Protein; 675 mg Sodium

Almost-Cobb Salad Wraps

With feta cheese replacing the Roquefort, this delicious wrap combines most of the ingredients of a Cobb salad in a handy package.

Bacon slices, diced	4	4
Large hard-cooked eggs, chopped (see Note 1)	4	4
Romaine lettuce mix	1 1/3 cups	325 mL
Diced tomato	1 cup	250 mL
Deli turkey breast slices, julienned (see Note 2)	6 oz.	170 g
Crumbled feta cheese	1/2 cup	125 mL
Caesar dressing	1/2 cup	125 mL
Flour tortillas (9 inch, 22 cm, diameter)	4	4

Cook bacon in large frying pan on medium until crisp. Transfer with slotted spoon to paper towel-lined plate to drain. Cool.

Combine next 5 ingredients in large bowl.

Add dressing and bacon. Toss.

Spoon turkey mixture down centre of each tortilla. Fold bottom end of tortilla over filling. Fold in sides, leaving top end open. Secure with wooden pick. Makes 4 wraps.

1 wrap: 502 Calories; 33.8 g Total Fat (8.3 g Mono, 11.0 g Poly, 9.1 g Sat); 255 mg Cholesterol; 28 g Carbohydrate; 1 g Fibre; 23 g Protein; 1480 mg Sodium

Note 1: To make hard-cooked eggs, place eggs in single layer in saucepan. Add cold water until about 1 inch (2.5 cm) above eggs. Cover. Bring to a boil. Reduce heat to medium-low. Simmer for 10 minutes. Drain. Cover eggs with cold water. Change water each time it warms until eggs are cool enough to handle. Remove shells. You can do this while the bacon is cooking to save time.

Note 2: To julienne, cut into very thin strips that resemble matchsticks.

Greek Chicken Wraps

Moist chicken thigh meat combines with classic Greek flavours in a wrap fit to feed company.

Lemon juice	2 tbsp.	30 mL
Olive (or cooking) oil	2 tbsp.	30 mL
Dried oregano	1/2 tsp.	2 mL
Garlic clove, minced	1	1
(or 1/4 tsp., 1 mL, powder)		
Salt	1/4 tsp.	1 mL
Pepper	1/4 tsp.	1 mL
Boneless, skinless chicken thighs, halved	3/4 lb.	340 g
Chopped green pepper	1/2 cup	125 mL
Chopped tomato	1/2 cup	125 mL
Crumbled feta cheese	1/4 cup	60 mL
Finely chopped English cucumber	1/4 cup	60 mL
(with peel)		
Plain yogurt	1/4 cup	60 mL
Finely chopped onion	2 tbsp.	30 mL
Flour tortillas (9 inch, 22 cm, diameter)	4	4

Preheat oven to 375°F (190°C). Combine first 6 ingredients in small cup.

Place chicken in medium bowl. Add 2 tbsp. (30 mL) lemon juice mixture. Stir until coated. Arrange on greased baking sheet with sides. Cook in oven for about 7 minutes per side until internal temperature reaches 165°F (74°C). Transfer to cutting board. Let stand for about 5 minutes until cool enough to handle. Chop.

Meanwhile, combine next 6 ingredients in small bowl. Add remaining lemon mixture. Stir. Add chicken. Stir.

Spoon chicken mixture across centre of each tortilla. Fold sides over filling. Roll up from bottom to enclose. Makes 4 wraps.

1 wrap: 363 Calories; 19.6 g Total Fat (7.9 g Mono, 2.5 g Poly, 5.4 g Sat); 65 mg Cholesterol; 26 g Carbohydrate; 1 g Fibre; 21 g Protein; 706 mg Sodium

Pictured on page 18.

Ham and Veggie Burritos

The warm comfort of ham and melted cheese all wrapped up in a tortilla—
with vegetables!

Cooking oil	1 tsp.	5 mL
Chopped onion	3/4 cup	175 mL
Chopped green pepper	1/4 cup	60 mL
Chopped red pepper	1/4 cup	60 mL
Dried basil	1/2 tsp.	2 mL
Dried oregano	1/2 tsp.	2 mL
Dried crushed chilies	1/4 tsp.	1 mL
Tomato pasta sauce	1/2 cup	125 mL
Flour tortillas (9 inch, 22 cm, diameter)	4	4
Deli ham slices	8	8
Grated Mexican cheese blend	1 1/2 cups	375 mL

Cooking spray

Preheat oven to 425°F (220°C). Heat cooking oil in large frying pan on medium-high. Add next 6 ingredients. Cook for about 5 minutes, stirring often, until vegetables are softened.

Spread pasta sauce over each tortilla, almost to edge. Scatter onion mixture over pasta sauce. Arrange ham over top. Sprinkle with cheese. Fold in sides. Roll up from bottom to enclose filling. Arrange, seam-side down, on greased baking sheet with sides.

Spray tortillas with cooking spray. Cook in oven for about 10 minutes until golden. Makes 4 burritos.

1 burrito: 386 Calories; 20.2 g Total Fat (0.7 g Mono, 0.4 g Poly, 8.6 g Sat); 58 mg Cholesterol; 30 g Carbohydrate; 1 g Fibre; 21 g Protein; 1324 mg Sodium

Pictured on page 18.

Tuna Sweet Corn Melts

*The classic British sandwich filling and jacket potato topping, in a classic
North American setting—the tuna melt! Use the leftover corn in Chili Beef
Steaks, page 50.*

Cans of flaked light tuna in water (6 oz., 170 g, each), drained	2	2
Canned kernel corn, drained	1/2 cup	125 mL
Mayonnaise	2 tbsp.	30 mL
Sour cream	2 tbsp.	30 mL
Thinly sliced green onion	1 tbsp.	15 mL
Lemon juice	1 tsp.	5 mL
Salt	1/8 tsp.	0.5 mL
Pepper	1/8 tsp.	0.5 mL
Whole-wheat bread slices, toasted	4	4
Grated Cheddar cheese	1 cup	250 mL

Preheat broiler. Combine first 8 ingredients in medium bowl.

Arrange toast slices on ungreased baking sheet with sides. Spoon tuna
mixture over toast slices.

Sprinkle with cheese. Broil on centre rack in oven for about 5 minutes until
cheese is melted and tuna mixture is heated through. Makes 4 melts.

*1 melt: 380 Calories; 20.1 g Total Fat (3.8 g Mono, 1.5 g Poly, 8.5 g Sat); 73 mg Cholesterol;
17 g Carbohydrate; 2 g Fibre; 31 g Protein; 841 mg Sodium*

Easy Cheesy Quesadillas

A quick and filling lunch, snack or appetizer that will satisfy any cheese craving and have you dreaming of Mexico!

Block cream cheese, softened	1/2 cup	125 mL
Flour tortillas (9 inch, 22 cm, diameter)	4	4
Grated Mexican cheese blend	1 1/2 cups	375 mL
Thinly sliced green onion	1/4 cup	60 mL
Finely diced seeded tomato	3/4 cup	175 mL
Salt	1/4 tsp.	1 mL

Cooking spray

Preheat oven to 400°F (205°C). Spread cream cheese over each tortilla, almost to edge.

Sprinkle next 4 ingredients, in order given, over half of each tortilla. Fold tortillas in half to cover filling. Press down lightly. Arrange on greased baking sheet with sides.

Spray tortillas with cooking spray. Cook in oven for about 15 minutes until crisp and cheese is melted. Cuts into 4 wedges each, for a total of 16 wedges.

1 wedge: 101 Calories; 7.0 g Total Fat (0 g Mono, trace Poly, 3.9 g Sat); 17 mg Cholesterol; 6 g Carbohydrate; trace Fibre; 4 g Protein; 211 mg Sodium

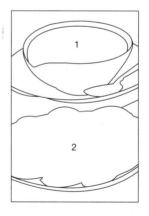

1. Curried Pea Soup, page 43
2. Tomato Feta Salad, page 37

Props: Sam & Squito

Tomato Feta Salad

A Greek twist on an Italian classic. Use the best tomatoes you can for the most flavourful results.

Olive (or cooking) oil	3 tbsp.	50 mL
Balsamic vinegar	2 tbsp.	30 mL
Dijon mustard	1/2 tsp.	2 mL
Dried basil	1/2 tsp.	2 mL
Salt	1/4 tsp.	1 mL
Pepper	1/4 tsp.	1 mL
Medium tomatoes, cut into 1/2 inch (12 mm) slices	4	4
Crumbled feta cheese	1/2 cup	125 mL
Finely chopped green onion	1 tbsp.	15 mL

Whisk first 6 ingredients in small bowl.

Arrange tomato in circular pattern around edge and in centre of serving plate. Drizzle 2 tbsp. (30 mL) olive oil mixture over top. Let stand for 25 minutes.

Sprinkle with cheese and green onion. Drizzle with remaining olive oil mixture. Serves 4.

1 serving: 181 Calories; 15.0 g Total Fat (8.4 g Mono, 1.6 g Poly, 4.3 g Sat); 17 mg Cholesterol; 9 g Carbohydrate; 1 g Fibre; 4 g Protein; 370 mg Sodium

Pictured on page 35.

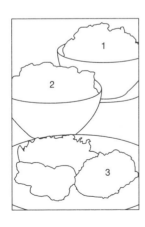

1. Creamy Curry Meatballs, page 49
2. Sweet Chili Pork, page 60
3. Dijon-Crusted Sirloin, page 47

Props: Loveplates

Roman Salad

This hearty salad balances flavours, textures and ingredients into a tasty dish that packs up well for lunches.

Olive oil	3 tbsp.	50 mL
Lemon juice	2 tbsp.	30 mL
White vinegar	2 tsp.	10 mL
Dried oregano	1/2 tsp.	2 mL
Salt	1/4 tsp.	1 mL
Pepper	1/4 tsp.	1 mL
Dried crushed chilies	1/8 tsp.	0.5 mL
Small garlic clove, minced	1	1
(or 1/8 tsp., 0.5 mL, powder)		
Can of chickpeas (garbanzo beans),	19 oz.	540 mL
rinsed and drained		
Diced tomato	2 cups	500 mL
Can of flaked light tuna in water, drained	6 oz.	170 g
Finely diced onion	2 tbsp.	30 mL

Whisk first 8 ingredients in large bowl.

Add remaining 4 ingredients. Stir. Makes about 5 cups (1.25 L).

1 cup (250 mL): 225 Calories; 11.2 g Total Fat (6.7 g Mono, 2.5 g Poly, 1.5 g Sat); 14 mg Cholesterol; 19 g Carbohydrate; 5 g Fibre; 14 g Protein; 365 mg Sodium

Salsa Chicken Soup

Sick days demand chicken soup, but with the added zest of your favourite salsa, you'll be tempted to play sick just to make some.

Water	3 cups	750 mL
Prepared chicken broth	2 cups	500 mL
Long-grain white rice	1/3 cup	75 mL
Cooking oil	1 tsp.	5 mL
Boneless, skinless chicken breast halves,	3/4 lb.	340 g
cut into 1/2 inch (12 mm) pieces		
Salt	1/4 tsp.	1 mL

(continued on next page)

Soups & Salads

| Frozen mixed vegetables | 1 cup | 250 mL |
| Salsa | 1 cup | 250 mL |

Combine first 3 ingredients in large saucepan. Bring to a boil. Reduce heat to medium. Simmer, covered, for about 15 minutes, stirring occasionally, until rice is tender.

Meanwhile, heat cooking oil in large frying pan on medium-high. Add chicken. Sprinkle with salt. Cook for about 5 minutes, stirring often, until chicken is no longer pink. Add to rice mixture.

Add vegetables and salsa. Stir. Cook, covered, for about 5 minutes until vegetables are tender. Makes about 6 cups (1.5 L).

1 cup (250 mL): 146 Calories; 2.0 g Total Fat (0.8 g Mono, 0.5 g Poly, 0.4 g Sat); 33 mg Cholesterol; 15 g Carbohydrate; trace Fibre; 15 g Protein; 790 mg Sodium

Pesto Chicken Noodle Soup

A boost of basil pesto adds flavour to this wholesome and hearty chicken noodle soup.

Prepared chicken broth	4 cups	1 L
Water	1 cup	250 mL
Medium egg noodles, broken up	3/4 cup	175 mL
Sliced carrot	3/4 cup	175 mL
Sliced celery	3/4 cup	175 mL
Cooking oil	2 tsp.	10 mL
Boneless, skinless chicken thighs, cut into 1/2 inch (12 mm) pieces	3/4 lb.	340 g
Chopped onion	1/2 cup	125 mL
Basil pesto	2 tbsp.	30 mL

Combine broth and water in large saucepan. Bring to a boil. Add next 3 ingredients. Stir. Reduce heat to medium. Boil gently, covered, for about 10 minutes until carrot is tender.

Meanwhile, heat cooking oil in large frying pan on medium-high. Add chicken and onion. Cook for about 5 minutes, stirring often, until onion is softened and chicken is no longer pink.

Add pesto. Stir. Add to broth mixture. Stir. Makes about 6 cups (1.5 L).

1 cup (250 mL): 179 Calories; 9.6 g Total Fat (2.9 g Mono, 1.8 g Poly, 2.0 g Sat); 44 mg Cholesterol; 10 g Carbohydrate; 1 g Fibre; 13 g Protein; 1092 mg Sodium

Raspberry Chicken Salad

Raspberry jam dresses the chicken and makes a speedy vinaigrette for this lovely meal salad.

Cooking oil	1/2 tsp.	2 mL
Boneless, skinless chicken breast halves, cut into 3/4 inch (2 cm) pieces	3/4 lb.	340 g
Raspberry jam	2 tbsp.	30 mL
Spring mix lettuce	4 cups	1 L
Sliced almonds, toasted (see Tip, below)	1/3 cup	75 mL
Sliced English cucumber (with peel), halved lengthwise before slicing	1/3 cup	75 mL
Thinly sliced celery	1/3 cup	75 mL
Sliced green onion	1/4 cup	60 mL
Cooking oil	2 tbsp.	30 mL
Balsamic vinegar	1 tbsp.	15 mL
Raspberry jam	1 tbsp.	15 mL
Salt	1/4 tsp.	1 mL
Pepper	1/8 tsp.	0.5 mL

Heat cooking oil in large frying pan on medium-high. Add chicken. Cook for about 5 minutes, stirring often, until chicken is no longer pink. Transfer to small bowl.

Add first amount of jam. Stir. Let stand for 10 minutes.

Meanwhile, toss next 5 ingredients in large bowl.

Combine remaining 5 ingredients in small cup. Drizzle over lettuce mixture. Add chicken mixture. Toss. Makes about 6 cups (1.5 L).

1 cup (250 mL): 172 Calories; 8.9 g Total Fat (5.0 g Mono, 2.4 g Poly, 0.8 g Sat); 33 mg Cholesterol; 9 g Carbohydrate; 1 g Fibre; 15 g Protein; 142 mg Sodium

 tip   When toasting nuts, seeds or coconut, cooking times will vary for each type of nut—so never toast them together. For small amounts, place ingredient in an ungreased shallow frying pan. Heat on medium for 3 to 5 minutes, stirring often, until golden. For larger amounts, spread ingredient evenly in an ungreased shallow pan. Bake in a 350°F (175°C) oven for 5 to 10 minutes, stirring or shaking often, until golden.

Warm Potato and Pea Salad

Sweet peas and crunchy celery provide taste and texture to this comfort-food salad. Serve warm or cold.

Baby potatoes, halved, larger ones quartered	1 1/2 lbs.	680 g
Salt	1/2 tsp.	2 mL
Cooking oil	1 tsp.	5 mL
Frozen peas	1 cup	250 mL
Thinly sliced celery	1/2 cup	125 mL
Sliced green onion	1/4 cup	60 mL
Sour cream	1/2 cup	125 mL
Bacon slices, cooked crisp and crumbled	4	4
Lemon juice	1 tbsp.	15 mL
Granulated sugar	1 tsp.	5 mL
Salt	1/4 tsp.	1 mL
Pepper	1/4 tsp.	1 mL

Pour water into large saucepan until about 1 inch (2.5 cm) deep. Add potato and salt. Cover. Bring to a boil. Reduce heat to medium. Boil gently for 12 to 15 minutes until tender. Drain. Transfer to large bowl. Cover to keep warm.

Heat cooking oil in medium frying pan on medium. Add next 3 ingredients. Heat and stir for 1 minute. Remove from heat.

Add remaining 6 ingredients. Stir. Add to potato. Stir well. Makes about 5 cups (1.25 L).

1 cup (250 mL): 231 Calories; 7.3 g Total Fat (1.5 g Mono, 0.5 g Poly, 3.6 g Sat); 22 mg Cholesterol; 32 g Carbohydrate; 4 g Fibre; 8 g Protein; 309 mg Sodium

Veggie Minestrone

This Italian soup staple is lunchtime fare at its hearty, chock-full-of-veggies best. Use the leftover black beans in a salad, stew or chili.

Cooking oil	2 tsp.	10 mL
Chopped onion	1/2 cup	125 mL
Chopped red pepper	1/2 cup	125 mL
Sliced fresh white mushrooms	1/2 cup	125 mL
Prepared beef broth	2 1/2 cups	625 mL
Can of diced tomatoes (with juice)	14 oz.	398 mL
Tomato sauce	3/4 cup	175 mL
Water	1/2 cup	125 mL
Salt	1/4 tsp.	1 mL
Pepper	1/8 tsp.	0.5 mL
Elbow macaroni	1/2 cup	125 mL
Canned black beans, rinsed and drained	1 cup	250 mL
Finely chopped green onion	2 tbsp.	30 mL
Grated Parmesan cheese, for garnish		

Heat cooking oil in large saucepan on medium. Add next 3 ingredients. Cook, uncovered, for about 8 minutes, stirring often, until onion is softened.

Add next 6 ingredients. Stir. Bring to a boil. Reduce heat to medium.

Add pasta. Stir. Boil gently, partially covered, for 6 to 8 minutes, stirring occasionally, until pasta is tender but firm.

Add beans. Stir.

Sprinkle with green onion and cheese. Makes about 6 cups (1.5 L).

1 cup (250 mL): 127 Calories; 2.4 g Total Fat (1.0 g Mono, 0.8 g Poly, 0.3 g Sat); 0 mg Cholesterol; 21 g Carbohydrate; 3 g Fibre; 6 g Protein; 1149 mg Sodium

Curried Pea Soup

A lovely green soup with a creamy texture and mild curry flavour. Perfectly balanced and suited to a cool day in need of brightening.

Butter	2 tbsp.	30 mL
Chopped onion	1 cup	250 mL
Curry powder	1 tbsp.	15 mL
Ground cumin	1 tsp.	5 mL
Ground ginger	1/2 tsp.	2 mL
Garlic cloves, minced	2	2
(or 1/2 tsp., 2 mL, powder)		
Salt	1 tsp.	5 mL
Pepper	1/2 tsp.	2 mL
Cayenne pepper	1/4 tsp.	1 mL
Frozen peas	5 cups	1.25 L
Prepared chicken broth	4 cups	1 L
Can of chickpeas (garbanzo beans), rinsed and drained	19 oz.	540 mL
Unsweetened applesauce	1 cup	250 mL
Brown sugar, packed	2 tsp.	10 mL
Plain yogurt	1/2 cup	125 mL
Lime juice	1 tbsp.	15 mL

Melt butter in Dutch oven on medium. Add next 8 ingredients. Cook, uncovered, for about 5 minutes, stirring often, until onion is softened.

Add next 5 ingredients. Stir. Bring to a boil. Reduce heat to medium. Cook, uncovered, for about 4 minutes, stirring occasionally, until peas are tender. Carefully process with hand blender, or in blender in batches, until smooth (see Safety Tip, below).

Add yogurt and lime juice. Stir. Makes about 9 1/2 cups (2.4 L).

1 cup (250 mL): 188 Calories; 4.6 g Total Fat (1.1 g Mono, 0.7 g Poly, 1.9 g Sat); 7 mg Cholesterol; 29 g Carbohydrate; 8 g Fibre; 9 g Protein; 1090 mg Sodium

Safety Tip: Follow manufacturer's instructions for processing hot liquids.

Pictured on page 35.

Dill Pasta Salad

Savoury ham and crunchy dill pickles complement each other well in a pasta salad perfect for a summer lunch or barbecue side.

Water	8 cups	2 L
Salt	1 tsp.	5 mL
Fusilli pasta	2 cups	500 mL
Chopped deli ham slices	1 cup	250 mL
Chopped red pepper	1 cup	250 mL
Thinly sliced celery	1/2 cup	125 mL
Mayonnaise	1/3 cup	75 mL
Chopped dill pickles	3 tbsp.	50 mL
Dried dillweed	1 tsp.	5 mL
Salt	1/4 tsp.	1 mL
Pepper	1/4 tsp.	1 mL
Grated Parmesan cheese	1/2 cup	125 mL

Combine water and salt in large saucepan. Bring to a boil. Add pasta. Boil, uncovered, for 7 to 9 minutes until tender but firm. Drain. Rinse with cold water. Drain well. Transfer to large bowl.

Add next 3 ingredients. Stir.

Combine next 5 ingredients in small bowl. Add to pasta mixture. Stir until coated.

Sprinkle with cheese. Stir. Makes about 4 1/2 cups (1.1 L).

1 cup (250 mL): 357 Calories; 18.2 g Total Fat (trace Mono, 0.1 g Poly, 4.5 g Sat); 35 mg Cholesterol; 32 g Carbohydrate; 2 g Fibre; 17 g Protein; 1003 mg Sodium

Fall Apple Salad

Make the most of the fall apple harvest with a simple vinaigrette that highlights fresh apples, tart cranberries and crunchy nuts.

Olive (or cooking) oil	2 tbsp.	30 mL
Balsamic vinegar	1 tbsp.	15 mL
Dijon mustard	1 tsp.	5 mL
Salt	1/4 tsp.	1 mL
Pepper	1/4 tsp.	1 mL

(continued on next page)

Romaine lettuce mix	8 cups	2 L
Thinly sliced unpeeled cooking apple (such as McIntosh)	1 1/2 cups	375 mL
Dried cranberries	1/2 cup	125 mL
Sliced almonds, toasted (see Tip, page 40)	1/2 cup	125 mL

Combine first 5 ingredients in small cup.

Combine remaining 4 ingredients in large bowl. Drizzle with olive oil mixture. Toss. Makes about 10 cups (2.5 L).

1 cup (250 mL): 92 Calories; 5.7 g Total Fat (3.7 g Mono, 1.1 g Poly, 0.6 g Sat); 0 mg Cholesterol; 10 g Carbohydrate; 2 g Fibre; 2 g Protein; 69 mg Sodium

Pictured on page 90 and on back cover.

Vegetarian Taco Salad

All the flavour of a great taco in a salad that makes a tasty meal or starter.

Sweet chili sauce	2 tbsp.	30 mL
Flour tortillas (9 inch, 22 cm, diameter)	2	2
Can of black beans, rinsed and drained	19 oz.	540 mL
Chopped tomato	1 cup	250 mL
Salsa	1/2 cup	125 mL
Diced green pepper	1/4 cup	60 mL
Sliced green onion	1/4 cup	60 mL
Sour cream	1/4 cup	60 mL
Lime juice	1 tbsp.	15 mL
Romaine lettuce mix	8 cups	2 L
Grated Mexican cheese blend	1 cup	250 mL

Preheat oven to 350°F (175°C). Spread chili sauce over each tortilla, almost to edge. Cut into 12 wedges each. Arrange, sauce-side up, in single layer on greased baking sheet with sides. Cook in oven for about 12 minutes until crisp and golden.

Meanwhile, combine next 7 ingredients in large bowl.

Add lettuce and cheese. Toss. Serve with tortilla wedges. Serves 4.

1 serving: 373 Calories; 15.0 g Total Fat (trace Mono, 1.3 g Poly, 7.3 g Sat); 35 mg Cholesterol; 41 g Carbohydrate; 10 g Fibre; 17 g Protein; 962 mg Sodium

Pictured on page 107.

Summery Tomato Soup

Tomato soup with some ginger heat—perfect for those long summer nights when you want a light yet flavourful and satisfying meal.

Cooking oil	2 tsp.	10 mL
Chopped onion	2 cups	500 mL
Chopped celery	1 cup	250 mL
Ground ginger	1/2 tsp.	2 mL
Garlic clove, minced	1	1
(or 1/4 tsp., 1 mL, powder)		
Pepper	1/4 tsp.	1 mL
Prepared chicken broth	4 cups	1 L
Can of diced tomatoes (with juice)	14 oz.	398 mL
Water	1 cup	250 mL
Can of tomato sauce	7 1/2 oz.	213 mL
Granulated sugar	2 tsp.	10 mL

Heat cooking oil in large saucepan on medium-high. Add onion and celery. Cook, uncovered, for about 7 minutes, stirring often, until softened.

Add next 3 ingredients. Heat and stir for about 1 minute until garlic is fragrant.

Add remaining 5 ingredients. Stir. Bring to a boil. Reduce heat to medium-low. Simmer, uncovered, for 10 minutes to blend flavours. Carefully process with hand blender, or in blender in batches, until smooth (see Safety Tip, below). Makes about 8 cups (2 L).

1 cup (250 mL): 62 Calories; 1.8 g Total Fat (0.9 g Mono, 0.6 g Poly, 0.2 g Sat); 0 mg Cholesterol; 10 g Carbohydrate; 1 g Fibre; 2 g Protein; 1039 mg Sodium

Safety Tip: Follow manufacturer's instructions for processing hot liquids.

Paré Pointer
She thought a paradox was two medical doctors.

Dijon-Crusted Sirloin

For a great meal, bake some baby potatoes while you cook up this well-spiced steak.

Olive (or cooking) oil	1 tbsp.	15 mL
Thinly sliced green onion	1/4 cup	60 mL
Garlic clove, minced	1	1
(or 1/2 tsp., 2 mL, powder)		
Dried oregano	1/2 tsp.	2 mL
Dried thyme	1/2 tsp.	2 mL
Cayenne pepper	1/8 tsp.	0.5 mL
Salt	1/8 tsp.	0.5 mL
Pepper	1/8 tsp.	0.5 mL
Fine dry bread crumbs	1/3 cup	75 mL
Olive (or cooking) oil	2 tsp.	10 mL
Montreal steak spice	1/2 tsp.	2 mL
Beef top sirloin steak	1 lb.	454 g
Dijon mustard	2 tbsp.	30 mL
Mayonnaise	2 tbsp.	30 mL

Preheat broiler. Heat first amount of olive oil in small frying pan on medium. Add next 7 ingredients. Cook for about 1 minute, stirring often, until garlic is fragrant. Remove from heat. Add bread crumbs. Stir.

Heat second amount of olive oil in large frying pan on medium-high. Sprinkle steak spice on both sides of steak. Add to frying pan. Cook for about 3 minutes per side until browned (see Note).

Meanwhile, combine mustard and mayonnaise in small cup. Spread over steak. Press bread crumb mixture over top. Broil on centre rack in oven for about 4 minutes until crust is browned and internal temperature reaches 145°F (63°C) for medium-rare or until steak reaches desired doneness (see Tip, page 118). Transfer to plate. Let stand for 5 minutes. Serves 4.

1 serving: 316 Calories; 19.9 g Total Fat (7.4 g Mono, 1.2 g Poly, 4.7 g Sat); 63 mg Cholesterol; 7 g Carbohydrate; 1 g Fibre; 26 g Protein; 403 mg Sodium

Pictured on page 36.

Note: This cooking time will produce a final steak doneness of medium-rare. If you like your steak more well-done, reduce heat and increase cooking time when frying on stovetop.

Lemon Pork Chops

Lively lemon adds zest to a delicate sauce served over tender pork.

All-purpose flour	2 tbsp.	30 mL
Dried oregano	1/2 tsp.	2 mL
Salt	1/4 tsp.	1 mL
Pepper	1/8 tsp.	0.5 mL
Boneless fast-fry pork chops	1 lb.	454 g
Butter	1 tbsp.	15 mL
Olive (or cooking) oil	1 tbsp.	15 mL
Prepared chicken broth	1 cup	250 mL
Finely chopped green onion	1/4 cup	60 mL
Lemon juice	2 tbsp.	30 mL
Grated lemon zest (see Tip, below)	1 tsp.	5 mL

Combine first 4 ingredients in medium shallow dish.

Press both sides of pork chops into flour mixture until coated. Reserve any remaining flour mixture.

Heat butter and olive oil in large frying pan on medium-high. Add pork chops. Cook for about 2 minutes per side until browned and no longer pink inside. Transfer to serving plate. Cover to keep warm.

Add reserved flour mixture to same frying pan. Heat and stir for 1 minute. Slowly add broth, stirring constantly until boiling and thickened.

Add remaining 3 ingredients. Stir. Pour over pork chops. Serves 4.

1 serving: 244 Calories; 16.6 g Total Fat (7.7 g Mono, 1.5 g Poly, 6.0 g Sat); 68 mg Cholesterol; 4 g Carbohydrate; trace Fibre; 19 g Protein; 594 mg Sodium

 tip When a recipe calls for grated zest and juice, it's easier to grate the fruit first, then juice it. Be careful not to grate down to the pith (white part of the peel), which is bitter and best avoided.

Creamy Curry Meatballs

Carrot accents tender meatballs served in a sweet and fruity curry sauce.

Large egg, fork-beaten	1	1
Fine dry bread crumbs	1/2 cup	125 mL
Grated carrot	1/2 cup	125 mL
Curry powder	1/2 tsp.	2 mL
Salt	3/4 tsp.	4 mL
Pepper	1/4 tsp.	1 mL
Lean ground beef	1 lb.	454 g
Unsweetened applesauce	1/4 cup	60 mL
Apricot jam	3 tbsp.	50 mL
Curry powder	1 tsp.	5 mL
Cayenne pepper, just a pinch		
Sour cream	1/2 cup	125 mL
Sliced green onion	1 tbsp.	15 mL

Preheat oven to 400°F (205°C). Combine first 6 ingredients in large bowl.

Add beef. Mix well. Roll into balls, using 1 tbsp. (15 mL) for each. Arrange in single layer on greased baking sheet with sides. Cook in oven for about 10 minutes until no longer pink inside. Makes about 42 meatballs.

Meanwhile, combine next 4 ingredients in large saucepan. Cook on medium for about 5 minutes, stirring often, until jam is melted and mixture is heated through.

Add sour cream. Stir until smooth. Add meatballs. Stir until coated. Transfer to serving bowl.

Sprinkle with green onion. Makes about 3 cups (750 mL).

1/2 cup (125 mL): 268 Calories; 12.3 g Total Fat (3.2 g Mono, 0.3 g Poly, 5.6 g Sat); 108 mg Cholesterol; 16 g Carbohydrate; 1 g Fibre; 21 g Protein; 430 mg Sodium

Pictured on page 36.

Chili Beef Steaks

Got an unexpected crowd to feed? Wow them with these chili and corn-sauced steaks! Refrigerate the leftover corn for later use, or add it to Tuna Sweet Corn Melt, page 33.

Cooking oil	1 tsp.	5 mL
Beef top sirloin steak, cut into 4 pieces	1 lb.	454 g
Chili powder	1 tsp.	5 mL
Salt	1/2 tsp.	2 mL
Cooking oil	1/2 tsp.	2 mL
Chopped onion	1/4 cup	60 mL
Canned kernel corn, drained	3/4 cup	175 mL
Salsa	3/4 cup	175 mL

Heat first amount of cooking oil in large frying pan on medium-high. Sprinkle both sides of steaks with chili powder and salt. Add to frying pan. Cook for about 3 minutes per side until internal temperature reaches 145°F (63°C) for medium-rare or until steaks reach desired doneness. Transfer to serving plate. Cover to keep warm. Reduce heat to medium.

Add second amount of cooking oil to same frying pan. Add onion. Cook for about 3 minutes, stirring often, until starting to brown.

Add corn and salsa. Stir. Cook for about 2 minutes, stirring occasionally, until heated through. Spoon over steaks. Serves 4.

1 serving: 243 Calories; 10.1 g Total Fat (4.3 g Mono, 0.8 g Poly, 3.2 g Sat); 60 mg Cholesterol; 9 g Carbohydrate; 1 g Fibre; 25 g Protein; 641 mg Sodium

Pork With Tomato Jam

Pork… and fruit! With a little ginger heat and some citrus sparkle, this jam complements the tender pork to perfection.

Cooking oil	1 tsp.	5 mL
Pork tenderloin, trimmed of fat, cut into 1/2 inch (12 mm) slices	1 lb.	454 g
Salt, sprinkle		
Pepper, sprinkle		

(continued on next page)

Can of diced tomatoes (with juice)	14 oz.	398 mL
Grated peeled cooking apple (such as McIntosh)	3/4 cup	175 mL
Brown sugar, packed	1/2 cup	125 mL
Lime juice	2 tbsp.	30 mL
Ground ginger	3/4 tsp.	4 mL

Heat cooking oil in large frying pan on medium. Add pork. Sprinkle with salt and pepper. Cook for about 4 minutes per side until browned and no longer pink inside. Transfer to serving plate. Cover to keep warm.

Add remaining 5 ingredients to same frying pan. Stir. Bring to a boil. Boil gently, uncovered, for about 10 minutes, stirring occasionally, until reduced and thickened. Serve with pork. Serves 4.

1 serving: 281 Calories; 5.1 g Total Fat (2.4 g Mono, 0.8 g Poly, 1.4 g Sat); 74 mg Cholesterol; 35 g Carbohydrate; 1 g Fibre; 25 g Protein; 339 mg Sodium

Pot-Saver Spaghetti Dinner

You're in a hurry—why dirty more dishes? This tasty version of spaghetti features the savoury flavours of beef, bacon and tomato, and can be made in one pot from start to finish!

Lean ground beef	1 lb.	454 g
Chopped onion	1 cup	250 mL
Chopped bacon	1/4 cup	60 mL
Can of diced tomatoes (with juice)	14 oz.	398 mL
Tomato pasta sauce	1 1/2 cups	375 mL
Water	1 1/2 cups	375 mL
Dried basil	1 tsp.	5 mL
Montreal steak spice	3/4 tsp.	4 mL
Spaghetti, broken up (about 3 1/2 cups, 875 mL)	6 oz.	170 g

Combine first 3 ingredients in large frying pan on medium-high. Scramble-fry for about 10 minutes until onion is softened.

Add next 5 ingredients. Stir. Bring to a boil.

Add pasta. Stir. Reduce heat to medium. Boil gently, covered, for 10 to 12 minutes, stirring occasionally, until pasta is tender but firm. Makes about 6 cups (1.5 L).

1 cup (250 mL): 325 Calories; 11.1 g Total Fat (0.8 g Mono, 0.2 g Poly, 3.7 g Sat); 54 mg Cholesterol; 32 g Carbohydrate; 1 g Fibre; 23 g Protein; 639 mg Sodium

Saucy Stovetop Patties

For a change, serve up the hamburgers Salisbury steak-style! With rich mushroom gravy, this homey dish is sure to satisfy.

Large egg, fork-beaten	1	1
Fine dry bread crumbs	1/2 cup	125 mL
Finely chopped onion	1/4 cup	60 mL
Montreal steak spice	1 tsp.	5 mL
Lean ground beef	1 lb.	454 g
Cooking oil	2 tsp.	10 mL
Sliced fresh white mushrooms	1 cup	250 mL
Prepared beef broth	1 cup	250 mL
All-purpose flour	1 tbsp.	15 mL

Combine first 4 ingredients in large bowl.

Add beef. Mix well. Divide into 4 equal portions. Shape into 1/2 inch (12 mm) thick patties.

Heat cooking oil in large frying pan on medium-high. Add patties. Cook for about 3 minutes per side until browned. Transfer to plate. Cover to keep warm. Reduce heat to medium.

Add mushrooms to same frying pan. Cook for about 4 minutes, stirring occasionally, until browned.

Stir broth into flour in small bowl until smooth. Slowly add to mushrooms, stirring constantly until boiling and thickened. Reduce heat to medium-low. Add patties. Turn until coated. Simmer, covered, for about 5 minutes until beef is no longer pink inside. Serves 4.

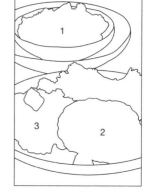

1 serving: 311 Calories; 15.8 g Total Fat (1.4 g Mono, 0.7 g Poly, 5.3 g Sat); 127 mg Cholesterol; 13 g Carbohydrate; 1 g Fibre; 27 g Protein; 688 mg Sodium

Pictured at right.

1. Mango Berry Crisp, page 139
2. Saucy Stovetop Patties, above
3. Pepper Cream Mashed Potatoes, page 130

Props: Sango

Cassoulet on Toast

You may think it'll take all day, but this quick and easy version of a tasty French classic will give you the stick-to-your ribs comfort of smoky pork and tender beans in just a few steps.

Pork breakfast sausages, cut into 1/2 inch (12 mm) pieces	8	8
Bacon slices, diced	8	8
Chopped onion	1 cup	250 mL
Garlic cloves, minced (or 3/4 tsp., 4 mL, powder)	3	3
Can of baked beans in tomato sauce	14 oz.	398 mL
Can of diced tomatoes (with juice)	14 oz.	398 mL
Whole-wheat bread slices, toasted	4	4

Cook sausage and bacon in large frying pan on medium for about 12 minutes, stirring occasionally, until sausage is browned and bacon is crisp. Transfer with slotted spoon to paper towel-lined plate to drain. Drain and discard all but 1 tsp. (5 mL) drippings.

Add onion and garlic to same frying pan. Cook for about 5 minutes, stirring often, until softened.

Add beans, tomatoes and sausage mixture. Stir. Bring to a boil. Boil gently, uncovered, for about 2 minutes, stirring occasionally, until heated through.

Place toast slices on 4 serving plates. Spoon bean mixture over top. Serve immediately. Serves 4.

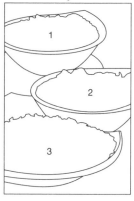

1 serving: 363 Calories; 15.3 g Total Fat (6.5 g Mono, 2.0 g Poly, 4.8 g Sat); 37 mg Cholesterol; 40 g Carbohydrate; 7 g Fibre; 18 g Protein; 1275 mg Sodium

1. Curried Pork and Peaches, page 65
2. West Indian Chicken Curry, page 79
3. Chicken Marrakesh, page 75

Props: Moderno

Creamy Mushroom Pork Chops

Dill and meaty mushrooms flavour a tangy sauce spooned over tender pork chops. Make sure to add mashed potato or noodles so you don't miss a drop.

Cooking oil	1 tsp.	5 mL
Boneless fast-fry pork chops (about 1 lb., 454 g)	4	4
Salt	1/4 tsp.	1 mL
Pepper	1/4 tsp.	1 mL
Cooking oil	1 tsp.	5 mL
Sliced fresh white mushrooms	2 cups	500 mL
Prepared chicken broth	1/2 cup	125 mL
Dried dillweed	1 tsp.	5 mL
Sour cream	1/4 cup	60 mL

Heat first amount of cooking oil in large frying pan on medium-high. Sprinkle both sides of pork chops with salt and pepper. Add to frying pan. Cook for about 2 minutes per side until browned and no longer pink inside. Transfer to serving plate. Cover to keep warm. Reduce heat to medium.

Add second amount of cooking oil to same frying pan. Add mushrooms. Cook for about 4 minutes, stirring occasionally, until mushrooms are browned.

Add broth and dillweed. Heat and stir for 1 minute. Remove from heat.

Add sour cream. Stir. Spoon over pork chops. Makes 4 pork chops.

1 pork chop: 229 Calories; 15.0 g Total Fat (5.7 g Mono, 1.5 g Poly, 5.6 g Sat); 70 mg Cholesterol; 2 g Carbohydrate; trace Fibre; 19 g Protein; 396 mg Sodium

Pictured on front cover.

Paré Pointer

His poodle swallowed a clock—now he's a watchdog.

Beef & Pork

Fireballs

A spicy, crunchy, versatile favourite that makes a great snack,
appetizer or dinner entree.

Large egg, fork-beaten	1	1
Quick-cooking rolled oats	1/4 cup	60 mL
Dried crushed chilies	1 tsp.	5 mL
Salt	1/4 tsp.	1 mL
Pepper	1/4 tsp.	1 mL
Lean ground beef	1 lb.	454 g
Fine dry bread crumbs	1/2 cup	125 mL
Montreal steak spice	1 1/2 tsp.	7 mL
Large egg, fork-beaten	1	1
Milk	2 tbsp.	30 mL

Cooking spray

Preheat broiler. Combine first 5 ingredients in large bowl.

Add beef. Mix well. Roll into balls, using 1 tbsp. (15 mL) for each.

Combine bread crumbs and steak spice in medium shallow dish.

Combine second egg and milk in small shallow dish. Dip meatballs into egg mixture. Roll in bread crumb mixture until coated. Discard any remaining egg mixture and bread crumb mixture. Arrange in single layer on greased baking sheet with sides.

Spray with cooking spray. Broil on top rack in oven for about 6 minutes until browned and no longer pink inside. Makes about 37 meatballs.

1 meatball: 32 Calories; 1.6 g Total Fat (0 g Mono, 0 g Poly, 0.6 g Sat); 20 mg Cholesterol; 1 g Carbohydrate; trace Fibre; 3 g Protein; 47 mg Sodium

Spicy Beef Noodles

When you're thinking take out but can't decide between Italian and Asian, why not eat faster (and better) than take out? Spaghetti with Asian flare is sure to appeal to everyone.

Water	12 cups	3 L
Salt	1 1/2 tsp.	7 mL
Spaghetti	8 oz.	225 g
Brown sugar, packed	3 tbsp.	50 mL
Lime juice	3 tbsp.	50 mL
Soy sauce	3 tbsp.	50 mL
Chili paste (sambal oelek)	1 tsp.	5 mL
Worcestershire sauce	1 tsp.	5 mL
Pepper	1/8 tsp.	0.5 mL
Cooking oil	1 tbsp.	15 mL
Sesame oil (for flavour)	1 tsp.	5 mL
Beef top sirloin steak, cut into thin strips	1 lb.	454 g
Thinly sliced red pepper	1/2 cup	125 mL
Green onions, cut into 2 inch (5 cm) pieces	6	6
Garlic cloves, minced (or 1/2 tsp., 2 mL, powder)	2	2

Combine water and salt in Dutch oven. Bring to a boil. Add pasta. Boil, uncovered, for 10 to 12 minutes, stirring occasionally, until tender but firm. Drain. Return to pot. Cover to keep warm.

Meanwhile, combine next 6 ingredients in small bowl.

Heat large frying pan or wok on medium-high until very hot. Add cooking and sesame oil. Add beef. Stir-fry for about 6 minutes until browned.

Add remaining 3 ingredients. Stir-fry for about 1 minute until red pepper is tender-crisp. Stir brown sugar mixture. Pour over beef mixture. Stir. Add pasta. Toss until coated. Makes about 7 cups (1.75 L).

1 cup (250 mL): 283 Calories; 7.9 g Total Fat (3.0 g Mono, 0.8 g Poly, 2.0 g Sat); 35 mg Cholesterol; 35 g Carbohydrate; 1.7 g Fibre; 19 g Protein; 621 mg Sodium

Peachy Mustard Pork

Pork and mustard get some help from peaches and apricot jam for a delicious and elegant dinner idea.

Pork tenderloin, trimmed of fat	1 lb.	454 g
Cooking oil	1 tsp.	5 mL
Salt	1/2 tsp.	2 mL
Pepper	1/4 tsp.	1 mL
Cooking oil	1/2 tsp.	2 mL
Chopped onion	1/4 cup	60 mL
Garlic clove, minced (or 1/4 tsp., 1 mL, powder)	1	1
Canned sliced peaches, drained and chopped	1/4 cup	60 mL
Prepared chicken broth	1/4 cup	60 mL
Apricot jam	2 tbsp.	30 mL
Dijon mustard	2 tbsp.	30 mL
Balsamic vinegar	2 tsp.	10 mL

Preheat gas barbecue to medium. Brush tenderloin with first amount of cooking oil. Sprinkle with salt and pepper. Cook on greased grill for about 20 minutes, turning occasionally, until internal temperature reaches 155°F (67°C). Transfer to cutting board. Cover with foil. Let stand for 5 minutes. Internal temperature should rise to at least 160°F (71°C). Cut into 1/2 inch (12 mm) slices. Cover to keep warm.

Meanwhile, heat second amount of cooking oil in small saucepan on medium. Add onion. Cook, uncovered, for 3 minutes, stirring often.

Add garlic. Heat and stir for about 2 minutes until onion is softened.

Add next 4 ingredients. Stir. Bring to a boil. Boil gently, uncovered, for 5 minutes to blend flavours. Carefully process in blender until almost smooth (see Safety Tip, below). Transfer to small bowl.

Add balsamic vinegar. Stir. Serve with pork. Serves 4.

1 serving: 195 Calories; 5.7 g Total Fat (2.8 g Mono, 1.0 g Poly, 1.5 g Sat); 74 mg Cholesterol; 11 g Carbohydrate; 1 g Fibre; 24 g Protein; 544 mg Sodium

Safety Tip: Follow manufacturer's instructions for processing hot liquids.

Sweet Chili Pork

A sweet and spicy stir-fry that'll have them asking for seconds! Serve with rice or egg noodles.

Sweet chili sauce	1/4 cup	60 mL
Soy sauce	2 tbsp.	30 mL
Cornstarch	1/2 tsp.	2 mL
Cooking oil	2 tsp.	10 mL
Pork tenderloin, trimmed of fat, halved lengthwise and cut crosswise into 1/4 inch (6 mm) slices	1 lb.	454 g
Cooking oil	1 tsp.	5 mL
Sliced orange pepper	1 cup	250 mL
Sliced celery	1/2 cup	125 mL
Green onions, cut into 1 inch (2.5 cm) pieces	4	4

Whisk first 3 ingredients in small bowl. Set aside.

Heat large frying pan or wok on medium-high until very hot. Add first amount of cooking oil. Add pork. Stir-fry for about 4 minutes until browned and no longer pink inside. Transfer to plate. Cover to keep warm.

Add second amount of cooking oil to same frying pan. Add orange pepper and celery. Stir-fry for about 2 minutes until vegetables are tender-crisp.

Add green onion and pork. Stir. Reduce heat to medium. Stir chili sauce mixture. Add to pork mixture. Heat and stir for about 1 minute until boiling and thickened. Makes about 3 cups (750 mL).

1/2 cup (125 mL): 144 Calories; 5.0 g Total Fat (2.5 g Mono, 1.0 g Poly, 1.1 g Sat); 49 mg Cholesterol; 7 g Carbohydrate; 1 g Fibre; 17 g Protein; 581 mg Sodium

Pictured on page 36.

Black Bean Chili

You've got just enough time to make a hearty and satisfying meal. For an easy side, pull biscuit mix from the pantry and prepare it while the chili cooks.

Lean ground beef	1 lb.	454 g
Bacon slices, chopped	2	2
Chopped celery	1 cup	250 mL
Chopped onion	1 cup	250 mL
Chili powder	2 tbsp.	30 mL
Ground cumin	1/2 tsp.	2 mL
Seasoned salt	1/2 tsp.	2 mL
Garlic clove, minced	1	1
(or 1/4 tsp., 1 mL, powder)		
Pepper	1/4 tsp.	1 mL
All-purpose flour	1 tbsp.	15 mL
Can of black beans, rinsed and drained	19 oz.	540 mL
Can of diced tomatoes (with juice)	14 oz.	398 mL
Frozen mixed vegetables	1 1/2 cups	375 mL
Prepared beef broth	1 cup	250 mL

Scramble-fry beef and bacon in Dutch oven on medium-high for about 7 minutes until starting to brown.

Add next 7 ingredients. Cook, uncovered, for 3 minutes, stirring often.

Sprinkle with flour. Heat and stir for 1 minute.

Add remaining 4 ingredients. Heat and stir, scraping any brown bits from bottom of pan, until boiling. Reduce heat to medium-low. Simmer, covered, for 8 minutes, stirring occasionally, to blend flavours. Makes about 6 cups (1.5 L).

1 cup (250 mL): 275 Calories; 9.4 g Total Fat (0.5 g Mono, 0.8 g Poly, 3.5 g Sat); 51 mg Cholesterol; 23 g Carbohydrate; 6 g Fibre; 23 g Protein; 927 mg Sodium

Maltaise Steaks

Pronounced mahl-TEESE, this delightful, orange-flavoured version of
hollandaise sauce gives your steak a gourmet touch in very little time.

Cooking oil	1 tbsp.	15 mL
Beef top sirloin steak, cut into 4 pieces	1 lb.	454 g
Salt	1/2 tsp.	2 mL
Pepper	1/4 tsp.	1 mL
Egg yolks (large), see Safety Tip below	2	2
Orange juice	1 tbsp.	15 mL
Lemon juice	1 tsp.	5 mL
Grated orange zest (see Tip, page 48)	1/2 tsp.	2 mL
Cayenne pepper, just a pinch		
Pepper, just a pinch		
Butter	1/2 cup	125 mL

Heat cooking oil in large frying pan on medium-high. Sprinkle both sides
of steak pieces with salt and pepper. Add to frying pan. Cook for about
3 minutes per side until internal temperature reaches 145°F (63°C) for
medium-rare or until beef reaches desired doneness. Transfer to serving
plate. Cover to keep warm.

Process next 6 ingredients in blender until smooth.

Place butter in small microwave-safe bowl. Microwave, uncovered, on high
(100%) for about 50 seconds until melted and bubbling. With motor
running, pour butter in thin stream through hole in blender lid until mixture
is thickened. Spoon over steaks. Serves 4.

1 serving: 436 Calories; 36.4 g Total Fat (12.1 g Mono, 2.5 g Poly, 18.5 g Sat); 223 mg Cholesterol;
1 g Carbohydrate; trace Fibre; 26 g Protein; 506 mg Sodium

Safety Tip: This recipe contains uncooked egg. Make sure to use fresh, clean
Grade A eggs. Keep chilled and consume the same day it is prepared.
Always discard leftovers. Pregnant women, young children or the elderly are
not advised to eat anything containing raw egg.

Chili Pork Chops

Dress up a breaded pork chop with a little chili heat and salsa to create a fast and zesty take on the classic chop.

All-purpose flour	3 tbsp.	50 mL
Chili powder	2 tsp.	10 mL
Seasoned salt	1/2 tsp.	2 mL
Large egg	1	1
Fine dry bread crumbs	2/3 cup	150 mL
Chili powder	1 tsp.	5 mL
Boneless fast-fry pork chops (about 1 lb., 454 g)	4	4
Cooking oil	1 tbsp.	15 mL
Salsa (optional)	1 cup	250 mL

Combine first 3 ingredients in medium shallow dish.

Beat egg with fork in small shallow dish.

Combine bread crumbs and second amount of chili powder in large shallow dish.

Press both sides of pork chops into flour mixture until coated. Dip into egg. Press both sides into bread crumb mixture until coated. Discard any remaining flour mixture, egg and bread crumb mixture.

Heat cooking oil in large frying pan on medium. Add pork chops. Cook for 3 to 4 minutes per side until browned and no longer pink inside.

Serve with salsa. Serves 4.

1 serving: 276 Calories; 15.2 g Total Fat (6.3 g Mono, 1.8 g Poly, 4.2 g Sat); 114 mg Cholesterol; 11 g Carbohydrate; 1 g Fibre; 22 g Protein; 254 mg Sodium

Pictured on page 125.

Microwave Meatloaf

The flavours of the Mediterranean from your microwave! Make sure your cover doesn't touch the fruity balsamic glaze.

Large egg, fork-beaten	1	1
Crumbled feta cheese	1 cup	250 mL
Fine dry bread crumbs	1/2 cup	125 mL
Finely chopped onion	1/2 cup	125 mL
Dried oregano	1/2 tsp.	2 mL
Seasoned salt	1/2 tsp.	2 mL
Pepper	1/4 tsp.	1 mL
Lean ground beef	1 lb.	454 g
Ketchup	1/2 cup	125 mL
Apricot jam	2 tbsp.	30 mL
Balsamic vinegar	1 tbsp.	15 mL

Combine first 7 ingredients in large bowl.

Add beef. Mix well. Shape into 7 inch (18 cm) round loaf. Place in greased glass 9 inch (22 cm) pie plate. Microwave, covered, on high (100%) for 8 minutes. Drain.

Meanwhile, combine remaining 3 ingredients in small bowl. Spread over meatloaf. Microwave, covered, on high (100%) for about 8 minutes until glaze is bubbling and internal temperature reaches 160°F (71°C). Let stand for 5 minutes. Cuts into 4 wedges.

1 wedge: 492 Calories; 22.2 g Total Fat (6.9 g Mono, 0.7 g Poly, 10.8 g Sat); 178 mg Cholesterol; 34 g Carbohydrate; 1 g Fibre; 38 g Protein; 1029 mg Sodium

Curried Pork and Peaches

Restless for dinner? Try this sweet curried pork over rice for a quick and colourful meal.

Cooking oil	1 tsp.	5 mL
Pork tenderloin, trimmed of fat, cut into 1/2 inch (12 mm) slices	1 lb.	454 g
Cooking oil	1 tsp.	5 mL
Chopped onion	1 cup	250 mL
All-purpose flour	1 tbsp.	15 mL
Curry powder	2 tsp.	10 mL
Salt	1/4 tsp.	1 mL
Can of diced tomatoes, drained	14 oz.	398 mL
Can of sliced peaches in juice, drained and juice reserved, chopped	14 oz.	398 mL
Reserved peach juice	1/2 cup	125 mL
Peach yogurt	1/2 cup	125 mL
Chopped green onion	1/4 cup	60 mL

Heat cooking oil in large frying pan on medium-high. Add pork. Cook for about 3 minutes per side until browned. Transfer to plate. Cover to keep warm.

Add second amount of cooking oil to same frying pan. Add onion. Cook for 2 minutes, stirring often.

Add next 3 ingredients. Heat and stir for about 1 minute until fragrant.

Add next 3 ingredients. Stir. Bring to a boil. Reduce heat to medium. Boil gently, uncovered, for about 5 minutes until thickened. Add pork. Heat and stir for about 1 minute until pork is no longer pink inside.

Add yogurt and green onion. Stir. Makes about 4 1/2 cups (1.1 L).

1 cup (250 mL): 287 Calories; 6.0 g Total Fat (2.8 g Mono, 1.0 g Poly, 1.5 g Sat); 67 mg Cholesterol; 34 g Carbohydrate; 3 g Fibre; 24 g Protein; 406 mg Sodium

Pictured on page 54.

Chicken Stew and Biscuits

Comfort food in minutes....and the half can of leftover soup can be used for tomorrow's lunch!

Biscuit mix	1 cup	250 mL
Milk	1/3 cup	75 mL
Grated Cheddar cheese	1/4 cup	60 mL
Cooking oil	2 tsp.	10 mL
Boneless, skinless chicken thighs, cut into 1 inch (2.5 cm) pieces	1 lb.	454 g
Salt	1/8 tsp.	0.5 mL
Pepper	1/8 tsp.	0.5 mL
Sliced fresh white mushrooms	2 cups	500 mL
Chopped onion	1/2 cup	125 mL
All-purpose flour	1 tbsp.	15 mL
Milk	1 1/2 cups	375 mL
Can of condensed cream of mushroom soup (10 oz., 284 mL)	1/2	1/2
Frozen peas	1/2 cup	125 mL
Basil pesto	2 tbsp.	30 mL

Preheat oven to 400°F (205°C). Stir first 3 ingredients in small bowl until just moistened. Drop batter in 8 mounds, about 1 inch (2.5 cm) apart, onto greased baking sheet with sides. Bake for about 10 minutes until wooden pick inserted in centre of biscuit comes out clean.

Meanwhile, heat cooking oil in large frying pan on medium-high. Add chicken. Sprinkle with salt and pepper. Cook for about 4 minutes, stirring often, until starting to brown.

Add mushrooms and onion. Cook for about 5 minutes, stirring often, until onions are softened.

Sprinkle with flour. Heat and stir for 1 minute.

Add remaining 4 ingredients. Stir. Bring to a boil, stirring constantly, until smooth. Cook, uncovered, for about 5 minutes, stirring often, until slightly reduced. Serve with biscuits. Serves 4.

1 serving: 490 Calories; 23.9 g Total Fat (5.7 g Mono, 2.7 g Poly, 6.6 g Sat); 92 mg Cholesterol; 36 g Carbohydrate; 2 g Fibre; 32 g Protein; 1000 mg Sodium

Pictured on page 71.

Turkey Feta Pizzas

Go ultra-thin for this pizza by using a tortilla as a base. Serve as a light meal or slice into wedges for a great starter.

Olive (or cooking) oil	1 tsp.	5 mL
Lean ground turkey	1/2 lb.	225 g
Garlic clove, minced	1	1
(or 1/4 tsp., 1 mL, powder)		
Dried oregano	1/4 tsp.	1 mL
Ground cinnamon, just a pinch		
Salt	1/8 tsp.	0.5 mL
Pepper, just a pinch		
Flour tortillas (9 inch, 22 cm, diameter)	2	2
Tomato sauce	1/4 cup	60 mL
Small green pepper, cut into thin rings	1	1
Crumbled feta cheese	1/2 cup	125 mL

Preheat oven to 475°F (240°C). Heat olive oil in large frying pan on medium-high. Add next 6 ingredients. Scramble-fry for about 6 minutes until turkey is browned and no longer pink.

Arrange tortillas on greased baking sheet with sides. Spread tomato sauce over each tortilla, almost to edge. Scatter turkey mixture over top. Arrange green pepper over turkey. Sprinkle with cheese. Cook on bottom rack in oven for about 7 minutes until edges are browned. Makes 2 pizzas.

1 pizza: 419 Calories; 21.4 g Total Fat (3.4 g Mono, 0.6 g Poly, 9.0 g Sat); 98 mg Cholesterol; 27 g Carbohydrate; 1 g Fibre; 31 g Protein; 1125 mg Sodium

Pictured on page 71.

Paré Pointer

What's a Greek urn? About 45 euros a day.

Coconut Mango Chicken

Mango salsa dances with a coconut-crusted chicken breast in a tango for the taste buds.

All-purpose flour	2 tbsp.	30 mL
Brown sugar, packed	1/4 tsp.	1 mL
Cayenne pepper	1/8 tsp.	0.5 mL
Salt	1/2 tsp.	2 mL
Pepper	1/8 tsp.	0.5 mL
Boneless, skinless chicken breast halves (4 – 6 oz., 113 g – 170 g, each)	4	4
Large egg	1	1
Medium unsweetened coconut	1 cup	250 mL
Cooking oil	1 tbsp.	15 mL
Chopped onion	1/4 cup	60 mL
Frozen mango pieces, chopped	2 cups	500 mL
Lime juice	2 tbsp.	30 mL
Brown sugar, packed	1 tbsp.	15 mL
Chili paste (sambal oelek)	1/2 tsp.	2 mL
Salt	1/4 tsp.	1 mL

Preheat oven to 425°F (220°C). Combine first 5 ingredients in large resealable freezer bag.

Add chicken. Toss until coated. Remove chicken. Discard any remaining flour mixture.

Beat egg with fork in large shallow dish.

Spread coconut on large plate. Dip chicken into egg. Press both sides into coconut until coated. Discard any remaining egg and coconut. Arrange chicken on greased baking sheet with sides. Cook in oven for about 18 minutes until internal temperature reaches 165°F (74°C) and coconut is golden.

Meanwhile, heat cooking oil in medium frying pan on medium-high. Add onion. Heat and stir for 2 minutes.

(continued on next page)

Add remaining 5 ingredients. Cook for about 2 minutes, stirring occasionally, until mango is softened. Serve with chicken. Serves 4.

1 serving: 357 Calories; 16.6 g Total Fat (2.9 g Mono, 1.5 g Poly, 10.5 g Sat); 102 mg Cholesterol; 25 g Carbohydrate; 4 g Fibre; 29 g Protein; 427 mg Sodium

Grilled Turkey Patties

These moist and flavourful patties are a nice change from traditional beef patties.

Large egg, fork-beaten	1	1
Chopped green onion	1/2 cup	125 mL
Chopped red pepper	1/2 cup	125 mL
Quick-cooking rolled oats	1/2 cup	125 mL
Barbecue sauce	2 tbsp.	30 mL
Salt	1/4 tsp.	1 mL
Pepper	1/8 tsp.	0.5 mL
Lean ground turkey	1 lb.	454 g
Cheddar cheese slices	4	4

Preheat gas barbecue to medium. Combine first 7 ingredients in large bowl.

Add turkey. Mix well. Divide into 4 equal portions. Shape into patties 4 inches (10 cm) in diameter (see Note). Cook on greased grill for about 5 minutes per side until internal temperature reaches 165°F (74°C) (see Tip below).

Place cheese on patties. Cook for about 1 minute until cheese is melted. Makes 4 patties.

1 patty: 337 Calories; 18.5 g Total Fat (2.7 g Mono, 0.4 g Poly, 8.4 g Sat); 149 mg Cholesterol; 10 g Carbohydrate; 2 g Fibre; 32 g Protein; 482 mg Sodium

Note: Because turkey patties are a little softer than beef burger patties, using parchment paper to transfer them to the grill or broiler keeps the patties intact and neater looking.

 Too cold to barbecue? Use the broiler instead! Your food should cook in about the same length of time—and remember to turn or baste as directed. Set your oven rack so that the food is about 3 to 4 inches (7.5 to 10 cm) away from the top element—for most ovens, this is the top rack.

Chic Cheddar Chicken

For truly chic bistro fare, serve this tasty chicken dish with a salad of baby greens dressed in a light vinaigrette.

Boneless, skinless chicken breast halves (4 – 6 oz., 113 g – 170 g, each), halved horizontally	4	4
Dijon mustard	2 tbsp.	30 mL
Mayonnaise	2 tbsp.	30 mL
Deli ham slices, halved	4	4
Thin tomato slices	16	16
Cheddar cheese slices, halved diagonally	8	8

Preheat broiler. Arrange chicken in single layer on greased baking sheet with sides.

Combine mustard and mayonnaise in small cup. Brush over chicken. Broil on top rack in oven for about 4 minutes until golden brown and no longer pink inside.

Layer next 3 ingredients, in order given, over chicken. Broil for about 1 minute until cheese is melted. Serves 8.

1 serving: 217 Calories; 13.0 g Total Fat (2.9 g Mono, 0.5 g Poly, 6.6 g Sat); 69 mg Cholesterol; 2 g Carbohydrate; trace Fibre; 22 g Protein; 434 mg Sodium

Pictured at right.

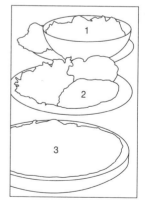

1. Chicken Stew and Biscuits, page 66
2. Chic Cheddar Chicken, above
3. Turkey Feta Pizza, page 67

Props: Danesco
Tabletop Lifestyles

Sweet Bruschetta Chicken

In the heat of summer, get some refreshment with this moist and tender chicken accompanied by a salsa with a sweet apple crunch.

Apricot jam	1 tbsp.	15 mL
Italian dressing	2 tbsp.	30 mL
Salt	1/8 tsp.	0.5 mL
Boneless, skinless chicken thighs	1 lb.	454 g
Chopped peeled cooking apple (such as McIntosh)	1/2 cup	125 mL
Chopped tomato	1/2 cup	125 mL
Chopped green onion	1/4 cup	60 mL
Italian dressing	1 tbsp.	15 mL
Salt, sprinkle		
Pepper, sprinkle		

Preheat gas barbecue to medium. Put jam into medium shallow microwave-safe bowl. Microwave, covered, on high (100%) for about 20 seconds until softened. Add dressing and salt. Stir.

Add chicken. Turn until coated. Marinate, covered, in refrigerator for 5 minutes. Remove chicken. Discard any remaining dressing mixture. Cook on greased grill for about 6 minutes per side until internal temperature reaches 165°F (74°C) (see Tip, page 69).

Meanwhile, combine remaining 6 ingredients in separate medium bowl. Serve with chicken. Serves 4.

1 serving: 214 Calories; 11.6 g Total Fat (3.3 g Mono, 2.0 g Poly, 2.8 g Sat); 74 mg Cholesterol; 6 g Carbohydrate; trace Fibre; 21 g Protein; 276 mg Sodium

Pictured on page 107.

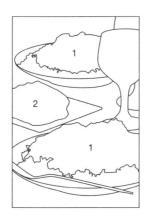

1. Pesto Chicken and Vegetables, page 85
2. Quick Company Cake, page 133

Lemon Garlic Chicken Noodles

Lemon, garlic, chicken and noodles. It'll have all the kids (even the big ones) rushing to the table.

Water	8 cups	2 L
Salt	1 tsp.	5 mL
Medium egg noodles	4 cups	1 L
Cooking oil	1 tbsp.	15 mL
Boneless, skinless chicken breasts, cut into 1 inch (2.5 cm) pieces	3/4 lb.	340 g
Garlic cloves, minced (or 1/2 tsp., 2 mL, powder)	2	2
Dried thyme	1/4 tsp.	1 mL
Salt	1/2 tsp.	2 mL
Pepper	1/4 tsp.	1 mL
All-purpose flour	1 tbsp.	15 mL
Prepared chicken broth	3/4 cup	175 mL
Grated Parmesan cheese	1/4 cup	60 mL
Roasted red peppers, chopped	1/4 cup	60 mL
Lemon juice	2 tbsp.	30 mL
Grated lemon zest (see Tip, page 48)	1/2 tsp.	2 mL

Combine water and salt in Dutch oven. Bring to a boil. Add noodles. Boil, uncovered, for 5 to 6 minutes, stirring occasionally, until tender but firm. Drain. Return to pot. Cover to keep warm.

Meanwhile, heat cooking oil in large frying pan on medium. Add next 5 ingredients. Cook for about 5 minutes, stirring often, until chicken starts to brown and is no longer pink inside.

Add flour. Heat and stir for 1 minute.

Slowly add broth, stirring constantly for about 1 minute until boiling and thickened.

Add remaining 4 ingredients. Heat and stir for about 1 minute until cheese is melted. Add to noodles. Stir. Makes about 6 cups (1.5 L).

1 cup (250 mL): 268 Calories; 6.8 g Total Fat (2.2 g Mono, 1.5 g Poly, 1.8 g Sat); 68 mg Cholesterol; 30 g Carbohydrate; 1 g Fibre; 21 g Protein; 601 mg Sodium

Chicken Marrakesh

Bring the casbah to your kitchen with this earthy and warm chicken and couscous dinner.

Olive (or cooking) oil	1 tbsp.	15 mL
Boneless, skinless chicken breast halves, cut into 1/4 inch (6 mm) slices	1 lb.	454 g
Salt	1/2 tsp.	2 mL
Pepper	1/8 tsp.	0.5 mL
Chopped red pepper	1 1/2 cups	375 mL
Sliced green onion	1/4 cup	60 mL
Ground cumin	1 1/2 tsp.	7 mL
Ground cinnamon	1/2 tsp.	2 mL
Ground ginger	1/2 tsp.	2 mL
Salt	1/2 tsp.	2 mL
Cayenne pepper	1/8 tsp.	0.5 mL
Water	1 3/4 cups	425 mL
Dried apricots, chopped	1/2 cup	125 mL
Orange juice	1/2 cup	125 mL
Couscous	1 cup	250 mL
Sliced almonds, toasted (see Tip, page 40)	1/4 cup	60 mL

Heat large frying pan or wok on medium-high until very hot. Add olive oil. Add chicken. Sprinkle with first amount of salt and pepper. Stir-fry for about 5 minutes until chicken is no longer pink inside. Transfer to plate. Cover to keep warm.

Add next 7 ingredients to same frying pan. Stir-fry for about 2 minutes until red pepper starts to soften.

Add next 3 ingredients. Stir. Bring to a boil.

Add couscous. Stir. Remove from heat. Let stand, covered, for 5 minutes. Fluff with fork. Add chicken. Stir.

Sprinkle with almonds. Makes about 5 1/2 cups (1.4 L).

1 cup (250 mL): 266 Calories; 6.8 g Total Fat (3.7 g Mono, 1.3 g Poly, 0.9 g Sat); 48 mg Cholesterol; 30 g Carbohydrate; 3 g Fibre; 24 g Protein; 487 mg Sodium

Pictured on page 54.

Turkey Alfredo

The creamy, homestyle comfort of alfredo sauce mixes with turkey, mushrooms, peas and peppers for the perfect sauce to serve over short noodles or mashed potatoes.

Cooking oil	1 tbsp.	15 mL
Lean ground turkey	1 lb.	454 g
Chopped onion	1/2 cup	125 mL
Chopped fresh white mushrooms	1 cup	250 mL
Frozen peas	1 cup	250 mL
Diced red pepper	1/2 cup	125 mL
Alfredo pasta sauce	1 3/4 cups	425 mL
Grated Parmesan cheese	1/4 cup	60 mL

Heat cooking oil in large frying pan on medium-high. Add turkey and onion. Scramble-fry for about 6 minutes until turkey is no longer pink.

Add next 3 ingredients. Stir. Cook for about 5 minutes, stirring occasionally, until red pepper is softened.

Add pasta sauce and cheese. Stir. Cook for about 2 minutes, stirring occasionally, until heated through. Makes about 4 cups (1 L).

1 cup (250 mL): 455 Calories; 30.6 g Total Fat (2.0 g Mono, 1.0 g Poly, 9.9 g Sat); 116 mg Cholesterol; 15 g Carbohydrate; 3 g Fibre; 30 g Protein; 867 mg Sodium

Chicken Nugget Dippers

Don't bother with the drive-through—you can make these chicken nuggets at home in less time than the round trip.

Large eggs	2	2
Fine dry bread crumbs	3/4 cup	175 mL
Montreal steak spice	1 1/2 tsp.	7 mL
Boneless, skinless chicken breast halves, cut into 1 1/2 inch (3.8 cm) pieces	1 lb.	454 g
Cooking spray		

(continued on next page)

Mayonnaise	1/2 cup	125 mL
Dijon mustard	2 tbsp.	30 mL
Liquid honey	2 tbsp.	30 mL

Preheat oven to 425°F (220°C). Beat eggs with fork in small shallow dish.

Combine bread crumbs and steak spice in medium shallow dish.

Dip chicken into egg. Press into crumb mixture until coated. Discard any remaining egg and bread crumb mixture. Arrange on greased baking sheet with sides. Spray with cooking spray. Cook in oven for about 15 minutes until no longer pink inside.

Meanwhile, combine remaining 3 ingredients in small bowl. Serve with chicken nuggets. Serves 4.

1 serving: 445 Calories; 25.7 g Total Fat (0.3 g Mono, 0.3 g Poly, 3.8 g Sat); 130 mg Cholesterol; 20 g Carbohydrate; 1 g Fibre; 30 g Protein; 613 mg Sodium

Sweet and Spicy Meatballs

A sweet pineapple-sauced meatball with kick! Great with noodles or rice.

Fine dry bread crumbs	3 tbsp.	50 mL
Sweet chili sauce	3 tbsp.	50 mL
Thinly sliced green onion	2 tbsp.	30 mL
Garlic powder	1/4 tsp.	1 mL
Salt	1/2 tsp.	2 mL
Pepper	1/4 tsp.	1 mL
Lean ground turkey	1 lb.	454 g
Can of pineapple tidbits (with juice)	14 oz.	398 mL
Sweet chili sauce	1/4 cup	60 mL
Cornstarch	1 tsp.	5 mL

Preheat broiler. Combine first 6 ingredients in medium bowl.

Add turkey. Mix well. Roll into balls, using 1 tbsp. (15 mL) for each. Arrange in single layer on greased baking sheet with sides. Broil on top rack in oven for about 7 minutes until no longer pink inside. Makes about 29 meatballs.

Meanwhile, process remaining 3 ingredients in blender or food processor until smooth. Transfer to medium saucepan. Bring to a boil on medium. Heat and stir for 1 minute. Add meatballs. Stir until coated. Makes about 3 1/2 cups (875 mL).

1/2 cup (125 mL): 151 Calories; 4.2 g Total Fat (0 g Mono, 0 g Poly, 1.1 g Sat); 37 mg Cholesterol; 16 g Carbohydrate; 1 g Fibre; 13 g Protein; 382 mg Sodium

Chicken Satay Stir-Fry

Stir-fry your chicken and vegetables and serve them over rice to satisfy your appetite.

Smooth peanut butter	1/3 cup	75 mL
Brown sugar, packed	1/4 cup	60 mL
Water	1/4 cup	60 mL
Lime juice	3 tbsp.	50 mL
Soy sauce	3 tbsp.	50 mL
Sesame oil	1 tbsp.	15 mL
Chili paste (sambal oelek)	1 tsp.	5 mL
Cornstarch	1 tsp.	5 mL
Garlic clove, minced	1	1
(or 1/4 tsp., 1 mL, powder)		
Cooking oil	1 tsp.	5 mL
Boneless, skinless chicken thighs,	3/4 lb.	340 g
cut into 1 inch (2.5 cm) pieces		
Cooking oil	1 tsp.	5 mL
Thinly sliced onion	1 cup	250 mL
Halved fresh white mushrooms	1 cup	250 mL
Thinly sliced celery	1 cup	250 mL
Thinly sliced red pepper	1 cup	250 mL
Medium unsweetened coconut	2 tbsp.	30 mL

Process first 9 ingredients in blender or food processor until smooth.

Heat large frying pan or wok on medium-high until very hot. Add cooking oil. Add chicken. Stir-fry for about 3 minutes until no longer pink inside. Transfer to plate. Cover to keep warm.

Add second amount of cooking oil to same frying pan. Add onion. Stir-fry for 2 minutes.

Add next 3 ingredients. Stir. Reduce heat to medium. Mix peanut butter mixture. Add to onion mixture. Cook for about 2 minutes, stirring often, until vegetables are tender-crisp and sauce is boiling and thickened. Add chicken. Stir. Cook for about 2 minutes, stirring occasionally, until heated through.

Sprinkle with coconut. Makes about 4 cups (1 L).

1 cup (250 mL): 412 Calories; 25.2 g Total Fat (3.9 g Mono, 2.2 g Poly, 6.1 g Sat); 56 mg Cholesterol; 29 g Carbohydrate; 3 g Fibre; 22 g Protein; 1198 mg Sodium

West Indian Chicken Curry

The warm flavour of cinnamon and the sweetness of sugar work in harmony with curry spices to make a delightful and satisfying chicken, potato and tomato curry.

Baby potatoes, halved	1/2 lb.	225 g
Cooking oil	2 tbsp.	30 mL
Chopped onion	2 cups	500 mL
Curry powder	2 tbsp.	30 mL
Brown sugar, packed	1 tbsp.	15 mL
Garlic cloves, minced	2	2
(or 1/2 tsp., 2 mL, powder)		
Salt	1/2 tsp.	2 mL
Pepper	1/2 tsp.	2 mL
Ground cinnamon	1/4 tsp.	1 mL
Cayenne pepper	1/8 tsp.	0.5 mL
Boneless, skinless chicken breast halves, cut into 1 inch (2.5 cm) pieces	1 lb.	454 g
Can of diced tomatoes (with juice)	14 oz.	398 mL
Plain yogurt	1/2 cup	125 mL

Pour water into small saucepan until about 1 inch (2.5 cm) deep. Add potato. Cover. Bring to a boil. Reduce heat to medium. Boil gently for 12 to 15 minutes until tender. Drain.

Meanwhile, heat cooking oil in large saucepan on medium-high. Add onion. Cook, uncovered, for 3 minutes, stirring often.

Add next 7 ingredients. Stir.

Add chicken. Stir. Reduce heat to medium. Cook, uncovered, for about 5 minutes, stirring occasionally, until chicken is browned.

Add tomatoes and potato. Heat and stir, scraping any brown bits from bottom of pan, until boiling. Reduce heat to medium-low. Cook, covered, for about 8 minutes, stirring occasionally, until heated through.

Add yogurt. Stir. Makes about 5 cups (1.25 L).

1 cup (250 mL): 261 Calories; 7.4 g Total Fat (3.6 g Mono, 2.0 g Poly, 1.0 g Sat); 55 mg Cholesterol; 24 g Carbohydrate; 2 g Fibre; 25 g Protein; 532 mg Sodium

Pictured on page 54.

Chicken Stroganoff

A family-friendly take on a classic. Make pasta night your favourite night!

Water	8 cups	2 L
Salt	1 tsp.	5 mL
Medium egg noodles	3 cups	750 mL
All-purpose flour	3 tbsp.	50 mL
Dried thyme	1/4 tsp.	1 mL
Salt	1/4 tsp.	1 mL
Pepper	1/4 tsp.	1 mL
Boneless, skinless chicken thighs, cut into 1 inch (2.5 cm) pieces	1 lb.	454 g
Cooking oil	1 tbsp.	15 mL
Chopped onion	1 cup	250 mL
Prepared chicken broth	1 cup	250 mL
Sliced fresh white mushrooms	1 cup	250 mL
Dijon mustard	1 tbsp.	15 mL
Garlic clove, minced (or 1/4 tsp., 1 mL, powder)	1	1
Salt	1/8 tsp.	0.5 mL
Sour cream	1/2 cup	125 mL

Combine water and salt in Dutch oven. Bring to a boil. Add noodles. Boil, uncovered, for 5 to 6 minutes, stirring occasionally, until tender but firm. Drain. Return to pot. Cover to keep warm.

Meanwhile, combine next 4 ingredients in large resealable freezer bag. Add chicken. Toss until coated. Remove chicken. Discard any remaining flour mixture.

Heat cooking oil in large saucepan on medium-high. Add chicken. Cook, uncovered, on medium-high for about 5 minutes, stirring occasionally, until browned.

Add onion. Cook for 3 minutes, stirring often.

Add next 5 ingredients. Heat and stir, scraping any brown bits from bottom of pan, until boiling. Reduce heat to medium-low. Cook, covered, for 10 minutes, stirring occasionally. Remove from heat.

(continued on next page)

Chicken & Turkey

Add sour cream and noodles. Stir. Makes about 7 cups (1.75 L).

1 cup (250 mL): 298 Calories; 13.5 g Total Fat (4.3 g Mono, 2.6 g Poly, 4.4 g Sat); 92 mg Cholesterol; 21 g Carbohydrate; 1 g Fibre; 21 g Protein; 375 mg Sodium

---

Turkey Tostadas

Slice these tasty tostadas into small wedges for a great appetizer—your guests will love the cumin and chili flavours. Try serving it with Corn and Black Bean Salsa, p. 150, which will help you use up the leftover corn and beans.

Cooking oil	2 tsp.	10 mL
Lean ground turkey	3/4 lb.	340 g
Chopped onion	1 cup	250 mL
Chili powder	1 tsp.	5 mL
Garlic powder	1/2 tsp.	2 mL
Ground cumin	1/2 tsp.	2 mL
Salt	1/2 tsp.	2 mL
Canned black beans, rinsed and drained	1 cup	250 mL
Canned kernel corn, drained	1 cup	250 mL
Salsa	1/2 cup	125 mL
Flour tortillas (9 inch, 22 cm, diameter)	4	4
Grated Mexican cheese blend (or Cheddar cheese)	1 cup	250 mL

Preheat oven to 450°F (230°C). Heat cooking oil in large frying pan on medium-high. Add next 6 ingredients. Scramble-fry for about 5 minutes until turkey is no longer pink.

Add black beans and corn. Heat and stir for 2 minutes.

Add salsa. Stir.

Arrange tortillas on 2 greased baking sheets with sides. Spread turkey mixture over each tortilla, almost to edge.

Sprinkle with cheese. Cook on separate racks in oven for about 10 minutes, switching position of baking sheets at halftime, until cheese is melted and edges are browned. Makes 4 tostadas.

1 tostada: 502 Calories; 21.7 g Total Fat (1.3 g Mono, 1.2 g Poly, 7.7 g Sat); 74 mg Cholesterol; 44 g Carbohydrate; 5 g Fibre; 30 g Protein; 1337 mg Sodium

Creamy Meatball Spaghetti

Tired of the same spaghetti and meatballs? Mix it up with chicken meatballs and a creamy sauce.

Water	12 cups	3 L
Salt	1 1/2 tsp.	7 mL
Spaghetti	8 oz.	225 g
Fine dry bread crumbs	1/2 cup	125 mL
Dried basil	1 tsp.	5 mL
Salt	1/2 tsp.	2 mL
Pepper	1/2 tsp.	2 mL
Lean ground chicken	1 lb.	454 g
Cooking oil	1/2 tsp.	2 mL
Chopped onion	1/2 cup	125 mL
Garlic clove, minced (or 1/4 tsp., 1 mL, powder)	1	1
Block cream cheese, cubed	4 oz.	125 g
Milk	1/2 cup	125 mL
Roasted red peppers, cut into strips	1/2 cup	125 mL
Chili paste (sambal oelek)	1 tsp.	5 mL
Salt	1/4 tsp.	1 mL
Pepper	1/4 tsp.	1 mL

Preheat broiler. Combine water and salt in Dutch oven. Bring to a boil. Add pasta. Boil, uncovered, for 10 to 12 minutes, stirring occasionally, until tender but firm. Drain, reserving 1 cup (250 mL) pasta water. Return pasta to same pot. Cover to keep warm.

Meanwhile, combine next 4 ingredients in medium bowl.

Add chicken. Mix well. Roll into balls, using 1 tbsp. (15 mL) for each. Arrange in single layer on greased baking sheet with sides. Broil on top rack in oven for about 7 minutes until no longer pink inside. Makes about 39 meatballs.

Heat cooking oil in large frying pan on medium. Add onion. Cook for about 5 minutes, stirring often, until onion is softened.

Add garlic. Heat and stir for about 30 seconds until fragrant.

(continued on next page)

Chicken & Turkey

Add remaining 6 ingredients, meatballs and reserved pasta water. Heat and stir until cheese is melted. Add to pasta. Toss until coated. Serve immediately. Makes about 8 cups (2 L).

1 cup (250 mL): 289 Calories; 10.6 g Total Fat (0.2 g Mono, 0.1 g Poly, 4.7 g Sat); 53 mg Cholesterol; 31 g Carbohydrate; 1 g Fibre; 16 g Protein; 514 mg Sodium

Breaded Chicken Patties

A beautifully breaded chicken patty that tastes great with a little mayonnaise and some fresh tomato slices.

Large egg, fork-beaten	1	1
Fine dry bread crumbs	1/2 cup	125 mL
Dried oregano	1/2 tsp.	2 mL
Dried thyme	1/4 tsp.	1 mL
Salt	1/2 tsp.	2 mL
Pepper	1/8 tsp.	0.5 mL
Lean ground chicken	1 lb.	454 g
Fine dry bread crumbs	1/3 cup	75 mL
Dried basil	1/2 tsp.	2 mL
Cooking oil	1 tbsp.	15 mL
Butter	2 tsp.	10 mL

Combine first 6 ingredients in large bowl.

Add chicken. Mix well. Divide into 4 equal portions. Shape into patties 4 inches (10 cm) in diameter.

Combine bread crumbs and basil in medium shallow bowl. Press both sides of patties into bread crumb mixture until coated. Discard any remaining bread crumb mixture.

Heat cooking oil and butter in large frying pan on medium. Add patties. Cook for about 5 minutes per side until golden and internal temperature reaches 165°F (74°C). Makes 4 patties.

1 patty: 284 Calories; 15.6 g Total Fat (2.5 g Mono, 1.1 g Poly, 4.0 g Sat); 80 mg Cholesterol; 15 g Carbohydrate; 1 g Fibre; 21 g Protein; 388 mg Sodium

Asian Chicken Noodles

Sesame soy noodles get festive with the added crunch of sweet red and yellow peppers.

Water	12 cups	3 L
Salt	1 1/2 tsp.	7 mL
Spaghetti	8 oz.	225 g
Cooking oil	1 tsp.	5 mL
Boneless, skinless chicken breast halves, cut into 1/2 inch (12 mm) pieces	1 lb.	454 g
Salt, sprinkle		
Pepper, sprinkle		
Soy sauce	1/3 cup	75 mL
Orange juice	1/4 cup	60 mL
Brown sugar, packed	2 tbsp.	30 mL
Sesame oil (for flavour)	1 tbsp.	15 mL
Ground ginger	1/2 tsp.	2 mL
Finely chopped red pepper	1/4 cup	60 mL
Finely chopped yellow pepper	1/4 cup	60 mL

Combine water and salt in Dutch oven. Bring to a boil. Add pasta. Boil, uncovered, for 10 to 12 minutes, stirring occasionally, until tender but firm. Drain. Return to pot. Cover to keep warm.

Meanwhile, heat cooking oil in large frying pan on medium-high. Add chicken. Sprinkle with salt and pepper. Cook for about 3 minutes, stirring often, until starting to brown.

Add next 5 ingredients. Bring to a boil. Reduce heat to medium-low. Simmer, uncovered, for about 6 minutes, stirring occasionally, until sauce is thickened and slightly reduced.

Add red and yellow pepper. Stir. Add to pasta. Toss. Makes about 6 cups (1.5 L).

1 cup (250 mL): 287 Calories; 4.8 g Total Fat (0.7 g Mono, 0.5 g Poly, 0.7 g Sat); 44 mg Cholesterol; 36 g Carbohydrate; 2 g Fibre; 24 g Protein; 1220 mg Sodium

Pesto Chicken and Vegetables

When the rush is on and the family's hungry, get it together with this versatile dish that pairs well with rice or pasta.

All-purpose flour	1/4 cup	60 mL
Salt	1/2 tsp.	2 mL
Pepper	1/4 tsp.	1 mL
Boneless, skinless chicken thighs (about 3 oz., 85 g, each), halved	6	6
Cooking oil	1 tbsp.	15 mL
Cooking oil	2 tsp.	10 mL
Sliced fresh white mushrooms	2 cups	500 mL
Chopped green pepper	1 cup	250 mL
Chopped onion	1 cup	250 mL
Can of diced tomatoes (with juice)	14 oz.	398 mL
Basil pesto	3 tbsp.	50 mL
Granulated sugar	1/2 tsp.	2 mL

Combine first 3 ingredients in large resealable freezer bag. Add chicken. Toss until coated. Remove chicken. Discard any remaining flour mixture.

Heat first amount of cooking oil in large frying pan on medium-high. Add chicken. Cook for 1 to 2 minutes per side until browned. Transfer to plate. Cover to keep warm.

Add second amount of cooking oil to same frying pan. Add next 3 ingredients. Cook for about 4 minutes, stirring often and scraping any brown bits from bottom of pan, until vegetables start to soften and brown.

Add remaining 3 ingredients and chicken. Stir. Bring to a boil. Reduce heat to medium-low. Simmer, covered, for about 10 minutes until chicken is no longer pink inside and vegetables are tender. Serves 4.

1 serving: 364 Calories; 21.4 g Total Fat (7.0 g Mono, 3.9 g Poly, 4.1 g Sat); 86 mg Cholesterol; 16 g Carbohydrate; 2 g Fibre; 27 g Protein; 597 mg Sodium

Pictured on page 72.

Salmon Souvlaki

We love this twist on traditional souvlaki, and we bet you will too! Serve as an appetizer or main course.

Lemon juice	2 tbsp.	30 mL
Olive (or cooking) oil	2 tbsp.	30 mL
Garlic clove, minced	1	1
(or 1/4 tsp., 1 mL, powder)		
Salt	1/4 tsp.	1 mL
Pepper	1/4 tsp.	1 mL
Plain yogurt	1/2 cup	125 mL
Finely chopped English cucumber	1/4 cup	60 mL
(with peel)		
Crumbled feta cheese	1 tbsp.	15 mL
Dried dillweed	1/2 tsp.	2 mL
Salmon fillets, skin and any	1 lb.	454 g
small bones removed, cut into		
1 inch (2.5 cm) pieces		
Dried oregano	1/2 tsp.	2 mL
Bamboo skewers (8 inches, 20 cm, each),	4	4
soaked in water for 10 minutes		

Preheat gas barbecue to medium-high. Combine first 5 ingredients in small cup.

Combine next 4 ingredients in small bowl. Add 1 tbsp. (15 mL) lemon juice mixture. Stir. Cover. Chill.

Put fish into medium bowl. Add oregano and remaining lemon juice mixture. Stir until coated. Marinate, covered, in refrigerator for 5 minutes. Remove fish. Discard any remaining lemon juice mixture.

Thread fish onto skewers. Cook on greased grill for about 3 minutes per side until fish flakes easily when tested with fork (see Tip, page 69). Serve with yogurt mixture. Serves 4.

1 serving: 277 Calories; 18.0 g Total Fat (8.9 g Mono, 3.9 g Poly, 4.9 g Sat); 61 mg Cholesterol; 3 g Carbohydrate; trace Fibre; 24 g Protein; 174 mg Sodium

Pictured on page 89.

Tuna Cakes

That can of tuna makes more than casseroles or sandwiches. These tender little cakes are a delicious main or appetizer, and the sauce can be used for dipping or spreading.

Large eggs, fork-beaten	2	2
Fine dry bread crumbs	1/2 cup	125 mL
Grated carrot	1/4 cup	60 mL
Grated Parmesan cheese	1/4 cup	60 mL
Roasted red peppers, finely chopped	1/4 cup	60 mL
Thinly sliced green onion	3 tbsp.	50 mL
Mayonnaise	1 tbsp.	15 mL
Cans of flaked light tuna in water (6 oz., 170 g, each), drained	2	2
Cooking oil	1 tbsp.	15 mL
Mayonnaise	1/4 cup	60 mL
Plain yogurt	1/4 cup	60 mL
Lemon juice	2 tsp.	10 mL
Dijon mustard	1 tsp.	5 mL

Combine first 7 ingredients in medium bowl.

Add tuna. Mix well. Divide into 8 equal portions. Shape into 1/2 inch (12 mm) thick patties.

Heat cooking oil in large frying pan on medium. Add patties. Cook for about 3 minutes per side until golden brown.

Meanwhile, combine remaining 4 ingredients in small bowl. Serve with patties. Serves 4

1 serving: 415 Calories; 25.2 g Total Fat (2.7 g Mono, 2.0 g Poly, 5.2 g Sat); 158 mg Cholesterol; 15 g Carbohydrate; 1 g Fibre; 29 g Protein; 853 mg Sodium

Pictured on page 89.

Paré Pointer

No matter how good your ideas, they won't work unless you do.

Fiesta Shrimp Creole

You get a wonderful nutty flavour out of your roux by letting it brown, but don't take your eyes off of it because it burns quickly! Serve over rice to soak up all that tasty sauce.

All-purpose flour	2 tbsp.	30 mL
Cooking oil	2 tbsp.	30 mL
Chopped celery	1 cup	250 mL
Chopped green pepper	1 cup	250 mL
Garlic cloves, minced	2	2
(or 1/2 tsp., 2 mL, powder)		
Salsa	1 1/2 cups	375 mL
Water	1 cup	250 mL
Can of tomato sauce	7 1/2 oz.	213 mL
Dried crushed chilies	1/4 tsp.	1 mL
Uncooked medium shrimp	1 lb.	454 g
(peeled and deveined)		

Combine flour and oil in large saucepan. Heat and stir on medium for about 9 minutes until starting to turn brown.

Add next 3 ingredients. Cook for about 3 minutes, stirring often, until vegetables start to soften.

Add next 4 ingredients. Stir. Bring to a boil. Reduce heat to medium. Cook, covered, for about 5 minutes until vegetables are tender.

Add shrimp. Stir. Cook, covered, for about 3 minutes until shrimp turn pink. Makes about 6 1/2 cups (1.6 L).

1 cup (250 mL): 157 Calories; 5.6 g Total Fat (2.7 g Mono, 1.7 g Poly, 0.6 g Sat); 106 mg Cholesterol; 10 g Carbohydrate; 1 g Fibre; 15 g Protein; 514 mg Sodium

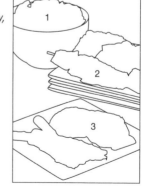

1. Shrimp Black Bean Stew, page 92
2. Salmon Souvlaki, page 86
3. Tuna Cakes, page 87

Props: the cellar

Cranberry-Crusted Salmon

The tang of cranberries and the zing of lemon contrast beautifully in the buttery crust on this salmon fillet.

Fine dry bread crumbs	1/2 cup	125 mL
Butter, melted	2 tbsp.	30 mL
Chopped dried cranberries	2 tbsp.	30 mL
Lemon juice	1 tbsp.	15 mL
Finely chopped green onion	1 1/2 tsp.	7 mL
Salt, sprinkle		
Pepper, sprinkle		
Salmon fillets, skin and any small bones removed	1 lb.	454 g

Preheat oven to 450°F (230°C). Combine first 7 ingredients in small bowl.

Arrange fillets on greased baking sheet with sides. Press bread crumb mixture onto fillets. Cook in oven for about 10 minutes until crust is golden and fish flakes easily when tested with fork. Serves 4.

1 serving: 381 Calories; 25.3 g Total Fat (10.5 g Mono, 5.4 g Poly, 7.6 g Sat); 72 mg Cholesterol; 13 g Carbohydrate; 1 g Fibre; 25 g Protein; 199 mg Sodium

Pictured at left and on back cover.

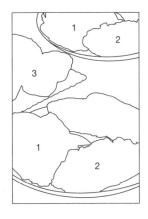

1. Fall Apple Salad, page 44
2. Cranberry-Crusted Salmon, above
3. Cranberry Coconut Brownies, page 137

Props: Sango

Shrimp Black Bean Stew

A southwestern-style chili for seafood lovers. Try this one served with toast for dipping.

Olive (or cooking) oil	2 tsp.	10 mL
Chopped onion	1/2 cup	125 mL
Chili powder	1 tbsp.	15 mL
Granulated sugar	1 tsp.	5 mL
Dried crushed chilies	1/4 tsp.	1 mL
Garlic clove, minced	1	1
(or 1/4 tsp., 1 mL, powder)		
Salt	1/4 tsp.	1 mL
Quartered baby potatoes	2 cups	500 mL
Water	2 tsp.	10 mL
Can of diced tomatoes (with juice)	28 oz.	796 mL
Can of black beans, rinsed and drained	19 oz.	540 mL
Can of kernel corn, drained	7 oz.	199 mL
Prepared chicken broth	3/4 cup	175 mL
Uncooked medium shrimp	3/4 lb.	340 g
(peeled and deveined)		
Diced green pepper	1/4 cup	60 mL

Heat olive oil in large saucepan on medium. Add next 6 ingredients. Cook for about 5 minutes, stirring often, until onion is softened.

Meanwhile, put potato into medium microwave-safe bowl. Add water. Microwave, covered, on high (100%), for about 8 minutes until tender. Cover to keep warm.

Add next 4 ingredients to onion mixture. Stir. Bring to a boil. Reduce heat to medium. Boil gently, partially covered, for 5 minutes.

Add shrimp and green pepper. Stir. Cook, covered, for about 3 minutes until shrimp turn pink. Add potato. Stir. Makes about 8 cups (2 L).

1 cup (250 mL): 191 Calories; 2.8 g Total Fat (1.0 g Mono, 1.0 g Poly, 0.3 g Sat); 65 mg Cholesterol; 26 g Carbohydrate; 5 g Fibre; 15 g Protein; 823 mg Sodium

Pictured on page 89.

Tuna Bread Crumb Fusilli

In days past, bread crumbs were often used as a cheese substitute by the peasants of southern Italy. This tuna and pasta dish has lemon freshness, and a delightful heat that sneaks up on you. It even makes a nice side dish for beef.

Water	16 cups	4 L
Salt	2 tsp.	10 mL
Fusilli pasta	4 cups	1 L
Olive (or cooking) oil	2 tbsp.	30 mL
Garlic cloves, minced	2	2
Dried crushed chilies	1/2 tsp.	2 mL
Salt	1/2 tsp	2 mL
Pepper	1/2 tsp.	2 mL
Can of flaked light tuna in water, drained	6 oz.	170 g
Lemon juice	3 tbsp.	50 mL
Thinly sliced green onion	2 tbsp.	30 mL
Fine dry bread crumbs	1/4 cup	60 mL
Butter, melted	2 tbsp.	30 mL

Combine water and salt in large pot. Bring to a boil. Add pasta. Boil, uncovered, for 7 to 9 minutes, stirring occasionally, until tender but firm. Drain. Return to pot. Cover to keep warm.

Meanwhile, heat olive oil in large frying pan on medium. Add next 4 ingredients. Heat and stir for about 1 minute until garlic is fragrant.

Add next 3 ingredients. Cook for about 3 minutes, stirring occasionally, until heated through. Remove from heat. Add pasta. Toss.

Add bread crumbs and butter. Toss until coated. Serve immediately. Makes about 8 cups (2 L).

1 cup (250 mL): 260 Calories; 7.9 g Total Fat (3.4 g Mono, 0.9 g Poly, 2.5 g Sat); 16 mg Cholesterol; 35 g Carbohydrate; 2 g Fibre; 11 g Protein; 272 mg Sodium

Apricot-Glazed Salmon

Salmon pairs beautifully with sweet glazes, and this easy balsamic and apricot reduction is no exception.

Apricot jam	1/3 cup	75 mL
Balsamic vinegar	1 tbsp.	15 mL
Garlic clove, minced	1	1
(or 1/4 tsp., 1 mL, powder)		
Ground ginger	1/4 tsp.	1 mL
Salmon fillets, skin and any small bones removed	1 lb.	454 g
Salt	1/8 tsp.	0.5 mL
Pepper	1/8 tsp.	0.5 mL

Preheat oven to 425°F (220°C). Combine first 4 ingredients in small frying pan. Bring to a boil. Reduce heat to medium-low. Simmer, uncovered, for about 5 minutes, stirring occasionally, until slightly thickened. Remove from heat. Cool slightly.

Sprinkle both sides of fillets with salt and pepper. Arrange on greased baking sheet with sides. Transfer 2 tbsp. (30 mL) jam mixture to small bowl. Brush over fillets (see Safety Tip, below). Cook in oven for 8 to 10 minutes until fish flakes easily when tested with fork. Brush with remaining jam mixture. Serves 4.

1 serving: 272 Calories; 11.9 g Total Fat (5.0 g Mono, 3.2 g Poly, 3.5 g Sat); 57 mg Cholesterol; 18 g Carbohydrate; trace Fibre; 23 g Protein; 138 mg Sodium

Safety Tip: Be sure to sanitize your brush after coating the raw salmon fillets. A second amount of jam mixture will be added once the fillets are cooked, so it is important that bacteria from the raw salmon do not contaminate the cooked salmon.

Broiled Italian Haddock

A beautiful medley of Italian vegetables and lovely fillets of perfectly cooked haddock. Elegant enough for company.

Olive (or cooking) oil	2 tsp.	10 mL
Chopped fresh white mushrooms	2 cups	500 mL
Chopped onion	1 cup	250 mL
Coarsely chopped green pepper	3/4 cup	175 mL
Coarsely chopped red pepper	3/4 cup	175 mL
Coarsely chopped yellow pepper	3/4 cup	175 mL
Balsamic vinegar	1 tbsp.	15 mL
Dried oregano	1/2 tsp.	2 mL
Salt	1/4 tsp.	1 mL
Pepper	1/4 tsp.	1 mL
Haddock fillets, any small bones removed	1 lb.	454 g
Basil pesto	2 tbsp.	30 mL
Grated Parmesan cheese	1/4 cup	60 mL

Preheat broiler. Heat olive oil in large frying pan on medium-high. Add mushrooms and onion. Cook for about 5 minutes, stirring often, until onion starts to soften and brown.

Add next 7 ingredients. Cook for about 3 minutes, stirring often, until peppers are tender-crisp.

Meanwhile, arrange fillets on greased baking sheet with sides. Spread pesto over fillets. Sprinkle with cheese. Broil on top rack in oven for about 4 minutes until cheese is browned and fish flakes easily when tested with fork. Serve with pepper mixture. Serves 4.

1 serving: 237 Calories; 9.6 g Total Fat (1.8 g Mono, 0.7 g Poly, 2.7 g Sat); 74 mg Cholesterol; 11 g Carbohydrate; 2 g Fibre; 27 g Protein; 423 mg Sodium

Paré Pointer

Knock knock. Who's there? Felix. Felix who? If Felix my ice cream again, I'll swat him.

Orange Almond Sole

We gave a sweet Spanish accent to the classic sole amandine. Segment the oranges over a bowl while the fish is cooking to capture any fresh juice. Serve with rice.

All-purpose flour	1/4 cup	60 mL
Salt	1/4 tsp.	1 mL
Pepper	1/8 tsp.	0.5 mL
Sole fillets, any small bones removed	1 lb.	454 g
Butter	2 tbsp.	30 mL
Medium oranges, segmented (see Note)	4	4
Orange juice	1/4 cup	60 mL
Garlic powder	1/4 tsp.	1 mL
Butter	2 tbsp.	30 mL
Grated orange zest (see Tip, page 48)	2 tsp.	10 mL
Salt, sprinkle		
Sliced almonds, toasted (see Tip, page 40)	1/4 cup	60 mL
Finely chopped green onion	2 tbsp.	30 mL

Combine first 3 ingredients in medium shallow dish.

Press both sides of fillets into flour mixture until coated. Discard any remaining flour mixture.

Melt half of first amount of butter in large frying pan on medium. Add fillets. Cook, in 2 batches, for about 2 minutes per side, adding remaining butter for second batch, until golden and fish flakes easily when tested with fork. Transfer to serving plate. Cover to keep warm.

Add next 3 ingredients to same frying pan. Stir. Bring to a boil.

Add next 3 ingredients. Heat and stir for about 30 seconds until butter is just melted. Spoon over fillets.

Scatter almonds and green onion over top. Serves 4.

1 serving: 341 Calories; 16.2 g Total Fat (5.4 g Mono, 1.6 g Poly, 7.8 g Sat); 85 mg Cholesterol; 29 g Carbohydrate; 8 g Fibre; 25 g Protein; 245 mg Sodium

Note: To segment citrus, trim a small slice of peel from both ends so the flesh is exposed. Place the fruit, cut-side down, on a cutting board. Remove the peel with a sharp knife, cutting down and around the flesh, leaving as little pith as possible. Over a small bowl, cut on either side of the membranes to release the segments.

Fish & Seafood

Orient Express Tuna

Say goodbye to tuna casserole. Here are tuna and noodles that are anything but boring.

Water	8 cups	2 L
Salt	1 tsp.	5 mL
Medium egg noodles	4 cups	1 L
Cooking oil	1 tbsp.	15 mL
Chopped fresh white mushrooms	1 1/2 cups	375 mL
Grated carrot	1 cup	250 mL
Sliced celery	3/4 cup	175 mL
Garlic cloves, minced	2	2
(or 1/2 tsp., 2 mL, powder)		
Water	1/2 cup	125 mL
Soy sauce	1/4 cup	60 mL
White vinegar	3 tbsp.	50 mL
Granulated sugar	2 tbsp.	30 mL
Sesame oil (for flavour)	1 tbsp.	15 mL
Cornstarch	1 tsp.	5 mL
Ground ginger	1 tsp.	5 mL
Dried crushed chilies	1/2 tsp.	2 mL
Cans of flaked light tuna in water	2	2
(6 oz., 170 g, each), drained		
Sliced green onion	1/3 cup	75 mL

Combine water and salt in Dutch oven. Bring to a boil. Add noodles. Boil, uncovered, for 5 to 6 minutes, stirring occasionally, until tender but firm. Drain. Return to pot. Cover to keep warm.

Meanwhile, heat cooking oil in large frying pan on medium-high. Add next 4 ingredients. Cook for about 5 minutes, stirring often, until softened. Reduce heat to medium.

Whisk next 8 ingredients in small bowl until sugar is dissolved. Add to vegetable mixture. Heat and stir until boiling and thickened.

Add tuna, green onion and noodles. Heat and stir for about 1 minute until heated through. Makes about 6 cups (1.5 L).

1 cup (250 mL): 298 Calories; 8.7 g Total Fat (2.4 g Mono, 1.9 g Poly, 1.4 g Sat); 54 mg Cholesterol; 35 g Carbohydrate; 2 g Fibre; 20 g Protein; 1123 mg Sodium

Curry Sole

Just add some steamed vegetables and rice and you've got a spicy and sweet dinner on the quick.

All-purpose flour	1/3 cup	75 mL
Salt	1/8 tsp.	0.5 mL
Sole fillets, any small bones removed	1 lb.	454 g
Cooking oil, divided	2 tsp.	10 mL
Cooking oil	1 tsp.	5 mL
Chopped onion	1/2 cup	125 mL
Curry powder	1/2 tsp.	2 mL
Garlic clove, minced	1	1
(or 1/4 tsp., 1 mL, powder)		
Dried crushed chilies	1/8 tsp.	0.5 mL
Ground cumin	1/8 tsp.	0.5 mL
Salt	1/4 tsp.	1 mL
Pepper	1/8 tsp.	0.5 mL
Prepared chicken broth	1/4 cup	60 mL
Unsweetened applesauce	1/4 cup	60 mL
Granulated sugar	1/2 tsp.	2 mL
Plain yogurt	1/2 cup	125 mL

Combine flour and salt in medium shallow bowl. Press both sides of fillets into flour mixture until coated. Discard any remaining flour mixture.

Heat 1 tsp. (5 mL) of first amount of cooking oil in large frying pan on medium. Add fillets. Cook, in 2 batches, for about 2 minutes per side, adding remaining cooking oil for second batch, until fish flakes easily when tested with fork. Transfer to serving plate. Cover to keep warm.

Heat second amount of cooking oil in same frying pan. Add next 7 ingredients. Reduce heat to medium-low. Cook for about 6 minutes, stirring often, until onion is softened.

Add next 3 ingredients. Cook for 2 to 3 minutes, stirring often, until heated through. Remove from heat.

Add yogurt. Stir. Pour over fillets. Serves 4.

1 serving: 202 Calories; 5.4 g Total Fat (2.3 g Mono, 1.4 g Poly, 0.9 g Sat); 57 mg Cholesterol; 13 g Carbohydrate; 1 g Fibre; 24 g Protein; 411 mg Sodium

Fish & Seafood

Presto Pesto Salmon Cakes

With a delicate, crisp exterior and moist, flavourful interior, these salmon cakes will transform those lowly cans of salmon into a feast.

Large egg, fork-beaten	1	1
Fine dry bread crumbs	1/4 cup	60 mL
Basil pesto	1 tbsp.	15 mL
Finely chopped onion	1 tbsp.	15 mL
Finely chopped red pepper	1 tbsp.	15 mL
Lemon juice	2 tsp.	10 mL
Garlic powder	1/8 tsp.	0.5 mL
Cans of pink salmon (6 1/2 oz., 184 g, each), drained, skin and round bones removed	2	2
Fine dry bread crumbs	1/4 cup	60 mL
Grated Parmesan cheese	2 tbsp.	30 mL
Pepper	1/4 tsp.	1 mL
Cayenne pepper, sprinkle		
Olive (or cooking) oil	1 tbsp.	15 mL
Lemon wedges, for garnish	8	8

Combine first 7 ingredients in medium bowl.

Add salmon. Mix well. Divide into 8 equal portions. Shape into 1/2 inch (12 mm) thick patties.

Combine next 4 ingredients in medium shallow bowl. Press both sides of patties into bread crumb mixture until coated. Discard any remaining bread crumb mixture.

Heat olive oil in large frying pan on medium. Add patties. Cook for about 4 minutes per side until golden brown.

Garnish with lemon wedges. Makes 8 cakes.

1 cake: 128 Calories; 7.5 g Total Fat (1.3 g Mono, trace Poly, 1.6 g Sat); 53 mg Cholesterol; 5 g Carbohydrate; trace Fibre; 11 g Protein; 294 mg Sodium

Seafood Gratin

Lovely fish and succulent shrimp in a creamy sauce. Serve with rice or pasta and colourful steamed veggies for a complete meal.

Alfredo pasta sauce	3/4 cup	175 mL
Caesar dressing	2 tbsp.	30 mL
Water	2 tbsp.	30 mL
Haddock fillets (4 – 5 oz., 113 – 140 g, each), any small bones removed, halved	2	2
Salmon fillets (4 – 5 oz., 113 – 140 g, each), skin and any small bones removed, halved	2	2
Uncooked medium shrimp (peeled and deveined)	1/4 lb.	113 g
Grated Parmesan cheese	1/3 cup	75 mL

Preheat broiler. Stir first 3 ingredients in small bowl until smooth.

Arrange haddock, salmon and shrimp in single layer in greased 9 x 9 inch (22 x 22 cm) pan. Spread pasta sauce mixture over top.

Sprinkle cheese over top. Broil on centre rack in oven for about 12 minutes until sauce is browned and bubbling and fish flakes easily when tested with fork. Serves 4.

1 serving: 342 Calories; 21.6 g Total Fat (3.6 g Mono, 4.3 g Poly, 7.2 g Sat); 133 mg Cholesterol; 3 g Carbohydrate; trace Fibre; 33 g Protein; 611 mg Sodium

Sunflower-Seeded Haddock

Sunflower seeds add a unique flavour and great crunch to moist and tender haddock.

Raw sunflower seeds, toasted (see Tip, page 40)	1/3 cup	75 mL
Butter, melted	2 tbsp.	30 mL
Fine dry bread crumbs	2 tbsp.	30 mL
Lemon juice	1 tsp.	5 mL
Garlic powder	1/8 tsp.	0.5 mL

(continued on next page)

Fish & Seafood

Haddock fillets, any small bones removed	1 lb.	454 g

Preheat oven to 400°F (205°C). Combine first 5 ingredients in small bowl.

Arrange fillets on greased baking sheet with sides. Press sunflower seed mixture onto fillets. Cook in oven for about 10 minutes until fish flakes easily when tested with fork. Serves 4.

1 serving: 243 Calories; 13.3 g Total Fat (1.6 g Mono, 0.5 g Poly, 4.4 g Sat); 80 mg Cholesterol; 5 g Carbohydrate; 1 g Fibre; 25 g Protein; 155 mg Sodium

Pantry Pirate's Pasta

Inspired by a traditional southern Italian pasta called spaghetti alla bucaniera, this recipe is a treasure.

Water	12 cups	3 L
Salt	1 1/2 tsp.	7 mL
Spaghetti	12 oz.	340 g
Olive oil	2 tbsp.	30 mL
Thinly sliced green onion	1/4 cup	60 mL
Garlic cloves, minced	2	2
Salt	1/4 tsp.	1 mL
Pepper	1/2 tsp.	2 mL
Dried crushed chilies	1/4 tsp.	1 mL
Uncooked medium shrimp (peeled and deveined)	3/4 lb.	340 g
Chopped tomato (3/4 inch, 2 cm, pieces)	3 cups	750 mL
Grated Parmesan cheese	1/4 cup	60 mL

Combine water and salt in Dutch oven. Bring to a boil. Add pasta. Boil, uncovered, for 10 to 12 minutes, stirring occasionally, until tender but firm. Drain. Return to pot. Cover to keep warm.

Meanwhile, heat olive oil in large frying pan on medium. Add next 5 ingredients. Heat and stir for about 1 minute until garlic is fragrant.

Add shrimp and tomato. Cook, covered, for about 5 minutes until shrimp turn pink. Add to pasta.

Add cheese. Toss until coated. Makes about 8 cups (2 L).

1 cup (250 mL): 265 Calories; 6.3 g Total Fat (2.6 g Mono, 0.9 g Poly, 1.4 g Sat); 68 mg Cholesterol; 36 g Carbohydrate; 2 g Fibre; 16 g Protein; 203 mg Sodium

Moroccan Bouillabaisse

Moroccan spices impart earthy flavour and warmth to this rich, brothy fish stew (BOOL-yah-bayz). Serve with flavourful whole-grain toast for a weekday meal or quick weekend lunch for company.

Cooking oil	2 tsp.	10 mL
Chopped onion	1 cup	250 mL
Chopped celery	3/4 cup	175 mL
Ground cumin	1 tsp.	5 mL
Ground cinnamon	1/2 tsp.	2 mL
Salt	1/2 tsp.	2 mL
Garlic clove, minced	1	1
(or 1/4 tsp., 1 mL, powder)		
Cayenne pepper	1/4 tsp.	1 mL
Ground allspice	1/8 tsp.	0.5 mL
Water	2 cups	500 mL
Can of diced tomatoes (with juice)	14 oz.	398 mL
Roasted red peppers, chopped	1/2 cup	125 mL
Tomato paste (see Note)	1 tbsp.	15 mL
Haddock fillets, any small bones removed, cut into 1 inch (2.5 cm) pieces	1/4 lb.	113 g
Salmon fillets, skin and any small bones removed, cut into 1 inch (2.5 cm) pieces	1/4 lb.	113 g
Sole fillets, any small bones removed, cut into 1 inch (2.5 cm) pieces	1/4 lb.	113 g
Uncooked medium shrimp (peeled and deveined)	1/4 lb.	113 g

Heat cooking oil in large saucepan on medium. Add next 8 ingredients. Cook for about 5 minutes, stirring often, until onion starts to soften.

Add next 4 ingredients. Stir. Bring to a boil. Reduce heat to medium. Boil gently, covered, for 5 minutes.

Add remaining 4 ingredients. Stir. Cook, covered, for about 5 minutes until fish flakes easily when tested with fork and shrimp turn pink. Makes about 7 cups (1.75 L).

(continued on next page)

1 cup (250 mL): 128 Calories; 3.7 g Total Fat (1.6 g Mono, 1.1 g Poly, 0.7 g Sat); 50 mg Cholesterol; 8 g Carbohydrate; 1 g Fibre; 14 g Protein; 511 mg Sodium

Note: Try freezing the tomato paste for 30 minutes before opening both ends and pushing the tube out. You'll be able to slice off what you need and wrap the rest for later.

Shrimp Omelette

When it's just the two of you and you want something quick and elegant, this simple and delicious omelette fits the bill. Serve with a tossed salad.

Butter	1 tbsp.	15 mL
Uncooked medium shrimp	1/2 lb.	225 g
(peeled and deveined)		
Chopped green onion	1 tbsp.	15 mL
Garlic clove, minced	1	1
(or 1/4 tsp., 1 mL, powder)		
Salt, just a pinch		
Pepper, just a pinch		
Large eggs	4	4
Salt	1/8 tsp.	0.5 mL
Cooking oil	1 tsp.	5 mL

Melt butter in medium non-stick frying pan on medium-high. Add next 5 ingredients. Cook for about 2 minutes, stirring often, until shrimp turn pink. Transfer to medium bowl. Cover to keep warm.

Beat eggs and second amount of salt with fork in small bowl.

Heat cooking oil in same frying pan on medium. Pour egg mixture into pan. Reduce heat to medium-low. When starting to set at outside edge, tilt pan and gently lift cooked egg mixture with spatula, easing around pan from outside edge in. Allow uncooked egg mixture to flow onto bottom of pan until egg is softly set. Scatter shrimp mixture over half of omelette. Fold omelette in half to cover shrimp mixture. Cook, covered, for about 1 minute until set and golden. Serves 2.

1 serving: 333 Calories; 19.0 g Total Fat (3.1 g Mono, 1.6 g Poly, 7.1 g Sat); 617 mg Cholesterol; 4 g Carbohydrate; trace Fibre; 35 g Protein; 484 mg Sodium

Lemon Salmon Fusilli

Pair healthy, delicious salmon with lemon, fusilli and vegetables for a quick and delicious meal.

Water	12 cups	3 L
Salt	1 1/2 tsp.	7 mL
Fusilli pasta	4 cups	1 L
Cooking oil	1 tsp.	5 mL
Salmon fillets, skin and any small bones removed, cut into 3/4 inch (2 cm) pieces	1 lb.	454 g
Alfredo pasta sauce	1 1/2 cups	375 mL
Frozen peas	2 cups	500 mL
Chopped red pepper	1/2 cup	125 mL
Lemon juice	3 tbsp.	50 mL

Combine water and salt in Dutch oven. Bring to a boil. Add pasta. Boil, uncovered, for 7 to 9 minutes, stirring occasionally, until tender but firm. Drain, reserving 1/2 cup (125 mL) pasta water. Return pasta to same pot. Cover to keep warm.

Meanwhile, heat cooking oil in large frying pan on medium-high. Add fish. Cook for about 3 minutes, turning occasionally, until browned. Transfer to plate. Cover to keep warm.

Add pasta sauce and reserved pasta water to same frying pan. Stir. Bring to a boil. Reduce heat to medium. Add peas. Cook for about 4 minutes, stirring occasionally, until peas are heated through.

Add red pepper, lemon juice and fish. Heat and stir for about 2 minutes until heated through. Add to pasta. Stir gently until coated. Makes about 10 cups (2.5 L).

1 cup (250 mL): 311 Calories; 12.0 g Total Fat (2.3 g Mono, 1.4 g Poly, 3.6 g Sat); 38 mg Cholesterol; 33 g Carbohydrate; 3 g Fibre; 16 g Protein; 275 mg Sodium

Pictured on page 107.

Paré Pointer

He's half that man's size—he's only his half brother.

Creamy Mushroom Spaghetti

Craving that rich, creamy alfredo taste but fresh out of canned sauce?
A few pantry staples can provide a great alternative. Adding Parmesan
cheese is optional.

Water	8 cups	2 L
Salt	1 tsp.	5 mL
Spaghetti	8 oz.	225 g
Butter	1 tbsp.	15 mL
Sliced fresh white mushrooms	3 cups	750 mL
Chopped onion	1/2 cup	125 mL
Milk	1/2 cup	125 mL
Caesar dressing	1/4 cup	60 mL
Dried thyme	1/2 tsp.	2 mL
Salt	1/4 tsp.	1 mL
Pepper	1/4 tsp.	1 mL
Sour cream	1/2 cup	125 mL

Combine water and salt in large saucepan. Bring to a boil. Add pasta. Boil, uncovered, for 10 to 12 minutes, stirring occasionally, until tender but firm. Drain, reserving 1/2 cup (125 mL) pasta water. Return pasta to same pot. Cover to keep warm.

Meanwhile, melt butter in large frying pan on medium-high. Add mushrooms and onion. Cook for about 5 minutes, stirring occasionally, until onion starts to brown.

Add next 5 ingredients. Heat and stir, scraping any brown bits from bottom of pan, until boiling. Reduce heat to medium. Cook for 5 minutes, stirring occasionally, to blend flavours. Remove from heat.

Add sour cream and reserved pasta water. Stir. Add to pasta. Stir. Serve immediately. Makes about 4 1/2 cups (1.1 L).

1 cup (250 mL): 365 Calories; 15.8 g Total Fat (2.5 g Mono, 4.4 g Poly, 6.0 g Sat);
26 mg Cholesterol; 44 g Carbohydrate; 2 g Fibre; 10 g Protein; 315 mg Sodium

Satay Tofu and Vegetables

Great satay richness surrounds soft tofu and tender-crisp veggies. Serve with rice so you don't miss out on any of the sauce. The leftover chickpeas make a good anytime snack, or a great addition to your next lunch salad.

Canned chickpeas (garbanzo beans), rinsed and drained	1 cup	250 mL
Water	1/2 cup	125 mL
Smooth peanut butter	1/4 cup	60 mL
Soy sauce	1/4 cup	60 mL
Balsamic vinegar	3 tbsp.	50 mL
Liquid honey	3 tbsp.	50 mL
Sesame oil (for flavour)	1 tbsp.	15 mL
Chili paste (sambal oelek)	1/2 tsp.	2 mL
Garlic powder	1/2 tsp.	2 mL
Package of medium tofu, cut into 1 inch (2.5 cm) cubes	1 lb.	454 g
Frozen Oriental mixed vegetables	6 cups	1.5 L

Process first 9 ingredients in blender or food processor until smooth.

Heat large frying pan on medium-high. Add tofu and chickpea mixture. Cook for about 3 minutes, stirring occasionally, until heated through.

Add vegetables. Stir. Cook, covered, for about 3 minutes until vegetables are tender-crisp. Makes about 6 cups (1.5 L).

1 cup (250 mL): 324 Calories; 15.2 g Total Fat (0.2 g Mono, 0.3 g Poly, 2.6 g Sat); trace Cholesterol; 33 g Carbohydrate; 4 g Fibre; 17 g Protein; 1554 mg Sodium

1. Lemon Salmon Fusilli, page 104
2. Vegetarian Taco Salad, page 45
3. Sweet Bruschetta Chicken, page 73

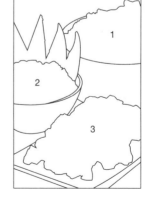

Thai Tofu Steaks

Tender tofu slices topped with a sweet, spicy peanut crust. Even tofu haters will like these flavours!

Cooking oil	1 tsp.	5 mL
Sesame oil (for flavour)	1 tsp.	5 mL
Package of medium tofu, cut crosswise into 8 slices	1 lb.	454 g
Salt, sprinkle		
Smooth peanut butter	2 tbsp.	30 mL
Sliced green onion	1 tbsp.	15 mL
Sweet chili sauce	1 tbsp.	15 mL
Soy sauce	1 tsp.	5 mL
Medium unsweetened coconut	3 tbsp.	50 mL
Sliced green onion	2 tbsp.	30 mL
Lime juice	1 tbsp.	15 mL

Preheat broiler. Heat cooking and sesame oil in large frying pan on medium-high. Add tofu. Sprinkle with salt. Cook for 3 to 4 minutes per side until starting to brown. Transfer to greased baking sheet with sides.

Stir next 4 ingredients in small bowl until smooth. Spread over tofu. Sprinkle with coconut. Broil on centre rack in oven for about 3 minutes until coconut is golden.

Sprinkle with second amount of green onion. Drizzle with lime juice. Makes 8 tofu steaks.

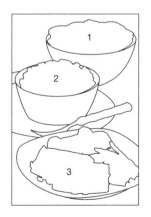

1 tofu steak: 81 Calories; 5.9 g Total Fat (0.7 g Mono, 1.1 g Poly, 1.8 g Sat); 0 mg Cholesterol; 4 g Carbohydrate; 1 g Fibre; 4 g Protein; 95 mg Sodium

Pictured at left.

1. Black Bean Stir-Fry, page 110
2. Mexi Mac and Cheese, page 110
3. Thai Tofu Steaks, above

Props: Moderno

Mexi Mac and Cheese

Looking for some creamy comfort food? Try this version of a pasta classic that adds black beans, salsa and Mexican cheese blend for some fiesta flair.

Water	12 cups	3 L
Elbow macaroni	3 cups	750 mL
Can of black beans, rinsed and drained	19 oz.	540 mL
Salsa	2 cups	500 mL
Can of kernel corn, drained	12 oz.	341 mL
Can of condensed cream of mushroom soup	10 oz.	284 mL
Chopped green pepper	1 cup	250 mL
Grated Mexican cheese blend	1 cup	250 mL

Bring water to a boil in Dutch oven. Add pasta. Boil, uncovered, for 8 to 10 minutes, stirring occasionally, until tender but firm. Drain. Return to pot. Cover to keep warm.

Meanwhile, combine next 5 ingredients in large saucepan. Bring to a boil on medium-high, stirring often. Add to pasta. Stir.

Sprinkle with cheese. Cover. Let stand for about 5 minutes until cheese is melted. Makes about 10 1/2 cups (2.6 L).

1 cup (250 mL): 271 Calories; 6.2 g Total Fat (0 g Mono, 0.4 g Poly, 2.2 g Sat); 11 mg Cholesterol; 41 g Carbohydrate; 5 g Fibre; 10 g Protein; 687 mg Sodium

Pictured on page 108.

Black Bean Stir-Fry

Black beans provide the backbone of a hearty stir-fry with zing. Serve over noodles or rice.

Water	1/2 cup	125 mL
Sweet chili sauce	3 tbsp.	50 mL
Frozen concentrated orange juice, thawed	2 tbsp.	30 mL
Soy sauce	2 tbsp.	30 mL
Cornstarch	1 tbsp.	15 mL
Cooking oil	2 tsp.	10 mL
Sesame oil (for flavour)	2 tsp.	10 mL
Thinly sliced onion	3/4 cup	175 mL

(continued on next page)

Vegetarian

| Frozen Oriental mixed vegetables | 6 cups | 1.5 L |
| Can of black beans, rinsed and drained | 19 oz. | 540 mL |

Whisk first 5 ingredients in small bowl until smooth.

Heat large frying pan or wok on medium-high until very hot. Add cooking and sesame oil. Add onion. Stir-fry for 2 minutes.

Add vegetables and beans. Stir-fry for about 4 minutes until vegetables are tender-crisp. Stir chili sauce mixture. Add to black bean mixture. Heat and stir for about 1 minute until boiling and thickened. Makes about 6 cups (1.5 L).

1 cup (250 mL): 221 Calories; 5.3 g Total Fat (0.9 g Mono, 1.1 g Poly, 0.6 g Sat); trace Cholesterol; 33 g Carbohydrate; 6 g Fibre; 9 g Protein; 1348 mg Sodium

Pictured on page 108.

Lentil Pipérade

Spicy lentils and a chunky tomato sauce modernize an ancient Basque dish (pronounced pee-pay-RAHD). Serve with rice, couscous, roasted potatoes or a fried egg.

Olive (or cooking) oil	1 tbsp.	15 mL
Chopped green pepper	1 cup	250 mL
Chopped onion	1 cup	250 mL
Chili powder	1 tsp.	5 mL
Dried thyme	1 tsp.	5 mL
Garlic cloves, minced	2	2
(or 1/2 tsp., 2 mL, powder)		
Ground cumin	1/2 tsp.	2 mL
Cayenne pepper	1/8 tsp.	0.5 mL
Salt	1/8 tsp.	0.5 mL
Can of lentils, rinsed and drained	19 oz.	540 mL
Can of diced tomatoes (with juice)	14 oz.	398 mL

Heat olive oil in large frying pan on medium. Add next 8 ingredients. Cook for about 8 minutes, stirring often, until onion starts to soften.

Add lentils and tomatoes. Stir. Bring to a boil. Reduce heat to medium-low. Simmer, covered, for about 5 minutes until heated through. Makes about 3 1/2 cups (875 mL).

1/2 cup (125 mL): 102 Calories; 2.1 g Total Fat (1.4 g Mono, 0.3 g Poly, 0.3 g Sat); 0 mg Cholesterol; 16 g Carbohydrate; 6 g Fibre; 6 g Protein; 287 mg Sodium

Vegetarian

Black Bean Burritos

Everyone can enjoy a bean burrito; it's Mexican comfort food.
Serve with tossed salad.

Cooking oil	1 tsp.	5 mL
Chopped green pepper	1 cup	250 mL
Chopped onion	1 cup	250 mL
Can of black beans, rinsed and drained	19 oz.	540 mL
Salsa	1 cup	250 mL
Can of kernel corn, drained	7 oz.	199 mL
Grated Mexican cheese blend	2 cups	500 mL
Flour tortillas (9 inch, 22 cm, diameter)	8	8
Salsa	1 cup	250 mL
Sour cream	1 cup	250 mL
Chopped green onion	1/4 cup	60 mL

Preheat oven to 425°F (220°C). Heat cooking oil in large frying pan on medium-high. Add green pepper and onion. Cook for 3 minutes, stirring often.

Add next 3 ingredients. Cook for about 2 minutes, stirring occasionally, until heated through and liquid is almost evaporated.

Sprinkle cheese across centre of each tortilla. Spoon black bean mixture over cheese. Fold sides over filling. Roll up from bottom to enclose. Arrange, seam-side down, on greased baking sheet with sides. Cook in oven for about 10 minutes until tortilla is golden and cheese is melted. Transfer to serving platter.

Top with remaining 3 ingredients. Makes 8 burritos.

1 burrito: 413 Calories; 19.4 g Total Fat (0.3 g Mono, 0.7 g Poly, 9.6 g Sat); 45 mg Cholesterol; 42 g Carbohydrate; 5 g Fibre; 14 g Protein; 1016 mg Sodium

Vegetarian

Spring Pesto Pasta

Spring-shaped pasta in a spring (primavera) sauce. Pesto is a classic Italian sauce traditionally made with basil, pine nuts, olive oil, garlic and Parmesan cheese.

Water	12 cups	3 L
Salt	1 1/2 tsp.	7 mL
Fusilli pasta	4 cups	1 L
Olive (or cooking) oil	1 tsp.	5 mL
Chopped green pepper	1 cup	250 mL
Chopped onion	1 cup	250 mL
Frozen Oriental mixed vegetables	3 cups	750 mL
Alfredo pasta sauce	2 cups	500 mL
Basil pesto	2 tbsp.	30 mL
Chopped tomato	1 cup	250 mL
Chopped green onion	1/2 cup	125 mL

Combine water and salt in Dutch oven. Bring to a boil. Add pasta. Boil, uncovered, for 7 to 9 minutes, stirring occasionally, until tender but firm. Drain. Return to pot. Cover to keep warm.

Meanwhile, heat olive oil in large frying pan on medium-high. Add green pepper and onion. Cook for about 5 minutes, stirring often, until onion is softened.

Add mixed vegetables. Stir. Cook for about 2 minutes, stirring occasionally, until tender-crisp.

Add pasta sauce and pesto. Stir. Cook for about 2 minutes, stirring occasionally, until heated through. Add to pasta.

Add tomato and green onion. Toss until coated. Makes about 9 cups (2.25 L).

1 cup (250 mL): 305 Calories; 12.4 g Total Fat (0.4 g Mono, 0.1 g Poly, 3.6 g Sat); 23 mg Cholesterol; 39 g Carbohydrate; 2 g Fibre; 8 g Protein; 521 mg Sodium

Jerk Lentil Patties

Combine exotic and spicy jerk spices in a crunchy, hearty lentil patty for a meal that's sure to impress your guests. Serve on buns or on their own with the tasty mango salsa.

Can of lentils, rinsed and drained	19 oz.	540 mL
Chopped onion	1/3 cup	75 mL
Frozen peas, thawed	1/4 cup	60 mL
Chili paste (sambal oelek)	1 tbsp.	15 mL
Brown sugar, packed	1 tsp.	5 mL
Dried thyme	1/2 tsp.	2 mL
Garlic cloves, halved	2	2
(or 1/2 tsp., 2 mL, powder)		
Ground allspice	1/2 tsp.	2 mL
Salt	1/4 tsp.	1 mL
Pepper	1/2 tsp.	2 mL
Ground cinnamon	1/4 tsp.	1 mL
Ground ginger	1/4 tsp.	1 mL
Large egg, fork-beaten	1	1
Quick-cooking rolled oats	1/2 cup	125 mL
Raw sunflower seeds, toasted	1/2 cup	125 mL
(see Tip, page 40)		
Olive (or cooking) oil	2 tbsp.	30 mL
Frozen mango pieces, thawed and drained, chopped	2 cups	500 mL
Lime juice	1 tbsp.	15 mL
Thinly sliced green onion	1 tbsp.	15 mL
Salt	1/8 tsp.	0.5 mL

Put first 12 ingredients into food processor. Process with on/off motion until lentils are mashed but not puréed. Transfer to medium bowl.

Add next 3 ingredients. Mix well. Divide into 8 equal portions. Shape into patties 3 inches (7.5 cm) in diameter.

Heat olive oil in large frying pan on medium. Add patties. Cook for about 5 minutes per side until browned.

(continued on next page)

Vegetarian

Meanwhile, combine remaining 4 ingredients in small bowl. Serve with patties. Serves 4.

1 serving: 424 Calories; 19.3 g Total Fat (5.1 g Mono, 1.1 g Poly, 2.4 g Sat); 54 mg Cholesterol; 48 g Carbohydrate; 15 g Fibre; 17 g Protein; 504 mg Sodium

Pictured on page 125.

Feta Chickpea Couscous

Mild Mediterranean flavours combine with feta, chickpeas, vegetables and a lemon zing for a satisfying and hearty meal or side.

Can of chickpeas (garbanzo beans), rinsed and drained	19 oz.	540 mL
Water	1 cup	250 mL
Lemon juice	1/4 cup	60 mL
Basil pesto	3 tbsp.	50 mL
Olive (or cooking) oil	1 tbsp.	15 mL
Grated lemon zest (see Tip, page 48)	1/2 tsp.	2 mL
Garlic powder	1/4 tsp.	1 mL
Salt	1/4 tsp.	1 mL
Couscous	1 1/4 cups	300 mL
Roasted red peppers, diced	1/3 cup	75 mL
Crumbled feta cheese	1/2 cup	125 mL
Diced tomato	1/2 cup	125 mL
Chopped green onion	1/4 cup	60 mL

Combine first 8 ingredients in large saucepan. Bring to a boil.

Add couscous and red peppers. Stir. Remove from heat. Let stand, covered, for 5 minutes. Fluff with fork.

Add remaining 3 ingredients. Stir. Makes about 7 cups (1.75 L).

1 cup (250 mL): 228 Calories; 9.2 g Total Fat (2.2 g Mono, 1.0 g Poly, 2.4 g Sat); 11 mg Cholesterol; 30 g Carbohydrate; 4 g Fibre; 9 g Protein; 424 mg Sodium

Chili Sin Carne

Everybody knows chili con carne (chili with meat). This is Chili Sin Carne (chili without meat). Fast, easy and tasty, this chili is perfect to put together quickly when you have unexpected company.

Olive (or cooking) oil	1 tbsp.	15 mL
Halved fresh white mushrooms	2 cups	500 mL
Diced onion	1 cup	250 mL
Diced celery	1/2 cup	125 mL
Chili powder	2 tbsp.	30 mL
Brown sugar, packed	1 tsp.	5 mL
Dried oregano	1 tsp.	5 mL
Ground cumin	1 tsp.	5 mL
Garlic cloves, minced	2	2
(or 1/2 tsp., 2 mL, powder)		
Salt	1/2 tsp.	2 mL
Pepper	1/2 tsp.	2 mL
Cayenne pepper	1/4 tsp.	1 mL
Can of black beans, rinsed and drained	19 oz.	540 mL
Can of chickpeas (garbanzo beans), rinsed and drained	19 oz.	540 mL
Can of diced tomatoes (with juice)	14 oz.	398 mL
Can of tomato sauce	14 oz.	398 mL
Can of kernel corn, drained	12 oz.	341 mL
Grated Cheddar cheese	1/2 cup	125 mL
Sour cream	1/2 cup	125 mL

Heat olive oil in Dutch oven on medium-high. Add next 3 ingredients. Cook, uncovered, for about 5 minutes, stirring often, until onion starts to brown. Reduce heat to medium.

Add next 8 ingredients. Heat and stir for about 1 minute until garlic is fragrant.

Add next 5 ingredients. Stir. Cook, covered, for about 10 minutes, stirring occasionally, until heated through.

Serve with cheese and sour cream. Makes about 8 2/3 cups (2.15 L).

1 cup (250 mL): 243 Calories; 8.0 g Total Fat (2.0 g Mono, 1.3 g Poly, 3.3 g Sat); 16 mg Cholesterol; 30 g Carbohydrate; 7 g Fibre; 11 g Protein; 940 mg Sodium

Vegetarian

Pasta Fagioli Stew

Minus the bacon, this traditional Italian stew (PAH-stah fa-ZHOH-lee) is a hearty meal that prepares in a single pot. Serve with crusty whole-grain bread.

Olive (or cooking) oil	1 tbsp.	15 mL
Chopped onion	1/2 cup	125 mL
Sliced carrot	1/2 cup	125 mL
Sliced celery	1/2 cup	125 mL
Dried basil	1 tsp.	5 mL
Dried oregano	1 tsp.	5 mL
Salt	3/4 tsp.	4 mL
Pepper	1/2 tsp.	2 mL
Garlic clove, minced	1	1
(or 1/4 tsp., 1 mL, powder)		
Can of baked beans in tomato sauce	14 oz.	398 mL
Can of diced tomatoes (with juice)	28 oz.	796 mL
Water	2 1/2 cups	625 mL
Tomato paste (see Note)	1 tbsp.	15 mL
Elbow macaroni	1 1/2 cups	375 mL
Grated Parmesan cheese	1/4 cup	60 mL

Heat olive oil in Dutch oven on medium. Add next 8 ingredients. Cook, uncovered, for about 5 minutes, stirring often, until onion starts to soften.

Meanwhile, put beans into small bowl. Mash half with fork until beans are just broken up. Add to onion mixture. Stir.

Add next 3 ingredients. Stir. Bring to a boil.

Add pasta. Reduce heat to medium. Boil gently, covered, for about 13 minutes, stirring often, until pasta is tender but firm.

Add cheese. Stir. Makes about 8 cups (2 L).

1 cup (250 mL): 184 Calories; 3.5 g Total Fat (1.3 g Mono, 0.3 g Poly, 1.0 g Sat); 4 mg Cholesterol; 32 g Carbohydrate; 4 g Fibre; 7 g Protein; 748 mg Sodium

Note: Try freezing the tomato paste for 30 minutes before opening both ends and pushing the tube out. You'll be able to slice off what you need and wrap the rest for later.

Mushroom Parmesan Frittata

For a simple and satisfying vegetarian weeknight meal, eat breakfast for dinner!

Olive (or cooking) oil	2 tsp.	10 mL
Diced onion	1 cup	250 mL
Sliced fresh white mushrooms	2 cups	500 mL
Dried thyme	1/4 tsp.	1 mL
Garlic clove, minced	1	1
(or 1/4 tsp., 1 mL, powder)		
Large eggs	6	6
Grated Parmesan cheese	1/4 cup	60 mL
Milk	1/4 cup	60 mL
Salt	1/4 tsp.	1 mL
Pepper	1/8 tsp.	0.5 mL
Grated Parmesan cheese	1/4 cup	60 mL

Preheat broiler. Heat olive oil in large non-stick frying pan on medium. Add onion. Cook for 3 minutes, stirring often.

Add next 3 ingredients. Cook for about 5 minutes, stirring often, until any liquid has evaporated.

Whisk next 5 ingredients in medium bowl. Pour over mushroom mixture. Reduce heat to medium-low. Cook, covered, for about 5 minutes until bottom is golden and top is almost set.

Sprinkle with second amount of cheese. Broil on centre rack in oven for about 3 minutes until cheese is melted and eggs are set (see Tip, below). Cuts into 4 wedges.

1 wedge: 218 Calories; 13.8 g Total Fat (1.7 g Mono, 0.4 g Poly, 5.7 g Sat); 338 mg Cholesterol; 8 g Carbohydrate; 1 g Fibre; 17 g Protein; 510 mg Sodium

 tip   When baking or broiling food in a frying pan with a handle that isn't ovenproof, wrap the handle in foil and keep it to the front of the oven, away from the element.

Sweet Curried Rice

This golden curry-flavoured rice with fruit accents will give your dinner some pizzazz.

Cooking oil	1 tbsp.	15 mL
Long-grain white rice	1 cup	250 mL
Curry powder	1 1/2 tsp.	7 mL
Salt	1/4 tsp.	1 mL
Water	2 cups	500 mL
Raisins	1/4 cup	60 mL
Liquid honey	2 tbsp.	30 mL
Lemon juice	1 tbsp.	15 mL
Salt	1/8 tsp.	0.5 mL
Chopped green onion	1/4 cup	60 mL
Sliced almonds, toasted (see Tip, page 40)	1/4 cup	60 mL

Heat cooking oil in medium saucepan on medium-high. Add next 3 ingredients. Heat and stir for about 1 minute until fragrant.

Add water and raisins. Stir. Bring to a boil. Reduce heat to medium-low. Simmer, covered, for 15 minutes, without stirring. Remove from heat. Let stand, covered, for about 5 minutes until rice is tender and liquid is absorbed. Fluff with fork.

Combine next 3 ingredients in small bowl. Add to rice. Stir.

Sprinkle with green onion and almonds. Makes about 3 1/2 cups (875 mL).

1/2 cup (125 mL): 186 Calories; 4.2 g Total Fat (2.5 g Mono, 1.1 g Poly, 0.4 g Sat); 0 mg Cholesterol; 34 g Carbohydrate; 1 g Fibre; 3 g Protein; 127 mg Sodium

Pictured on page 126.

Paré Pointer

Bad chickens use fowl play.

Vegetable Fried Rice

Make fried rice healthier by making it at home—in no time! The authentic flavours of this dish pair well with fish, chicken or beef.

Water	1 1/2 cups	375 mL
Long-grain white rice	1 cup	250 mL
Frozen Oriental mixed vegetables	2 cups	500 mL
Cooking oil	1 tsp.	5 mL
Sesame oil (for flavour)	1 tsp.	5 mL
Sliced green onion	1/4 cup	60 mL
Ground ginger	1 tsp.	5 mL
Garlic powder	1/2 tsp.	2 mL
Salt	1/4 tsp.	1 mL
Soy sauce	2 tbsp.	30 mL

Pour water into medium saucepan. Bring to a boil. Add rice. Stir. Reduce heat to medium-low. Simmer, covered, for 15 minutes, without stirring. Remove from heat. Let stand, covered, for about 5 minutes until rice is tender and liquid is absorbed. Fluff with fork. Cover to keep warm.

Meanwhile, put vegetables into medium microwave-safe bowl. Microwave, covered, on defrost (30%) for about 4 minutes until starting to thaw. Transfer to cutting board. Chop coarsely.

Heat large frying pan or wok on medium-high until very hot. Add cooking and sesame oil. Add next 4 ingredients and vegetables. Stir-fry for about 2 minutes until vegetables are tender-crisp.

Add rice and soy sauce. Stir-fry for about 1 minute until rice is coated. Transfer to serving dish. Makes about 4 cups (1 L).

1/2 cup (125 mL): 127 Calories; 1.7 g Total Fat (0.4 g Mono, 0.2 g Poly, 0.3 g Sat); trace Cholesterol; 24 g Carbohydrate; trace Fibre; 3 g Protein; 543 mg Sodium

Tunisian Couscous

If the idea of more rice or potatoes is boring you to tears, don't well up—get cooking. This exotic couscous pairs with any meat.

Water	1 3/4 cups	425 mL
Salt	1/4 tsp.	1 mL
Couscous	1 cup	250 mL
Olive (or cooking) oil	1 tbsp.	15 mL
Chopped onion	1 cup	250 mL
Finely diced carrot	1/4 cup	60 mL
Diced red pepper	1/2 cup	125 mL
Frozen peas	1/2 cup	125 mL
Brown sugar, packed	1 tsp.	5 mL
Ground cumin	1/2 tsp.	2 mL
Montreal steak spice	1/2 tsp.	2 mL
Garlic clove, minced	1	1
(or 1/4 tsp., 1 mL, powder)		
Ground cinnamon	1/4 tsp.	1 mL
Cayenne pepper	1/8 tsp.	0.5 mL
Lemon juice	2 tbsp.	30 mL

Combine water and salt in small saucepan. Bring to a boil. Add couscous. Stir. Remove from heat. Let stand, covered, for 5 minutes. Fluff with fork. Cover to keep warm.

Meanwhile, heat olive oil in large frying pan on medium. Add onion and carrot. Cook for about 5 minutes, stirring often, until onion is softened.

Add next 8 ingredients. Cook for about 3 minutes, stirring often, until garlic is fragrant and carrot is tender.

Add lemon juice and couscous. Stir. Makes about 4 cups (1 L).

1/2 cup (250 mL): 89 Calories; 2.1 g Total Fat (1.2 g Mono, 0.3 g Poly, 0.3 g Sat); 0 mg Cholesterol; 16 g Carbohydrate; 2 g Fibre; 3 g Protein; 130 mg Sodium

Pictured on page 126.

Italian Peas and Bacon

Trying to convince the kids to eat peas? Looking for a more elegant alternative for guests? Bacon, onion, red pepper and dressing add flair and flavour to plain peas.

Bacon slices, diced	4	4
Chopped onion	1/2 cup	125 mL
Frozen peas	2 cups	500 mL
Chopped red pepper	1/2 cup	125 mL
Italian dressing	2 tbsp.	30 mL

Cook bacon in large frying pan on medium for about 10 minutes, stirring occasionally, until crisp. Transfer with slotted spoon to paper towel-lined plate to drain. Drain and discard all but 1 tsp. (5 mL) drippings.

Add onion to same pan. Cook for about 4 minutes, stirring often, until onion is softened.

Add peas and red pepper. Cook for about 5 minutes, stirring occasionally, until peas are tender. Transfer to serving dish.

Add dressing and bacon. Stir. Makes about 3 1/4 cups (800 mL).

1/2 cup (125 mL): 90 Calories; 3.8 g Total Fat (1.0 g Mono, 0.3 g Poly, 1.0 g Sat); 5 mg Cholesterol; 10 g Carbohydrate; 3 g Fibre; 5 g Protein; 222 mg Sodium

Cumin Carrots and Corn

Brighten any dinner plate with this sunny colour combination of red, orange and yellow vegetables.

Sliced carrot	3 cups	750 mL
Cooking oil	2 tsp.	10 mL
Can of kernel corn, drained	7 oz.	199 mL
Diced red pepper	1/2 cup	125 mL
Ground cumin	1/2 tsp.	2 mL
Salt	1/4 tsp.	1 mL
Pepper, sprinkle		

(continued on next page)

Pour water into large saucepan until about 1 inch (2.5 cm) deep. Add carrot. Cover. Bring to a boil. Reduce heat to medium. Boil gently for about 8 minutes until carrot is tender-crisp. Drain. Return to pot. Cover to keep warm.

Meanwhile, heat cooking oil in large frying pan on medium-high. Add remaining 5 ingredients. Cook for about 5 minutes, stirring often, until red pepper is tender-crisp. Add carrot. Heat and stir for 1 minute. Makes about 4 cups (1 L).

1/2 cup (125 mL): 50.5 Calories; 1.5 g Total Fat (0.7 g Mono, 0.4 g Poly, 0.1 g Sat); 0 mg Cholesterol; 8 g Carbohydrate; 2 g Fibre; 1 g Protein; 174 mg Sodium

Orange Ginger Vegetables

This tasty and tangy side mixes well with rice and grilled meats for a well-balanced meal.

Cooking oil	1 tsp.	5 mL
Garlic clove, minced	1	1
(or 1/4 tsp., 1 mL, powder)		
Frozen concentrated orange juice, thawed	2 tbsp.	30 mL
Soy sauce	1 tbsp.	15 mL
White vinegar	1 tbsp.	15 mL
Brown sugar, packed	1 tsp.	5 mL
Ground ginger	1/4 tsp.	1 mL
Pepper	1/4 tsp.	1 mL
Frozen Oriental mixed vegetables	3 cups	750 mL

Heat cooking oil in large saucepan on medium. Add garlic. Heat and stir for about 1 minute until fragrant.

Add next 6 ingredients. Stir. Bring to a boil.

Add vegetables. Stir. Cook, covered, for 5 to 7 minutes, stirring occasionally, until tender-crisp. Makes about 2 cups (500 mL).

1/2 cup (125 mL): 95 Calories; 2.3 g Total Fat (0.7 g Mono, 0.4 g Poly, 0.3 g Sat); trace Cholesterol; 15 g Carbohydrate; 1 g Fibre; 3 g Protein; 751 mg Sodium

Pictured on page 125.

Spicy Roasted Vegetables

A little garlic, a little spice and some heat turn vegetables into a warming side dish that can go with almost anything, or can be eaten on its own. Perfect for a winter night.

Olive (or cooking) oil	1 tbsp.	15 mL
Balsamic vinegar	2 tsp.	10 mL
Chili paste (sambal oelek)	1/2 tsp.	2 mL
Garlic powder	1/2 tsp.	2 mL
Salt	1/8 tsp.	0.5 mL
Chopped carrot	1 1/2 cups	375 mL
Medium red peppers, cut into strips	2	2
Medium onion, cut into 8 wedges	1	1

Preheat oven to 450°F (230°C). Whisk first 5 ingredients in large bowl.

Add remaining 3 ingredients. Toss. Arrange in single layer on greased baking sheet with sides. Cook in oven for about 24 minutes, stirring at halftime, until tender-crisp and starting to brown. Makes about 3 cups (750 mL).

1/2 cup (125 mL): 53 Calories; 2.6 g Total Fat (1.7 g Mono, 0.4 g Poly, 0.4 g Sat); 0 mg Cholesterol; 8 g Carbohydrate; 2 g Fibre; 1 g Protein; 81 mg Sodium

Pictured at right.

1. Orange Ginger Vegetables, page 123
2. Chili Pork Chops, page 63
3. Spicy Roasted Vegetables, above
4. Jerk Lentil Patties, page 114

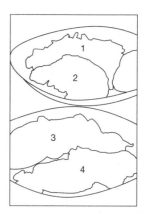

Mexican Pilaf

Sweet corn, meaty mushrooms and mild chili heat turn plain rice into a golden opportunity for a quick meal. Serve with chicken or as a filling for burritos.

Water	1 1/2 cups	375 mL
Long-grain white rice	1 cup	250 mL
Cooking oil	2 tsp.	10 mL
Sliced fresh white mushrooms	1 cup	250 mL
Chili powder	1 tsp.	5 mL
Ground cumin	1/2 tsp.	2 mL
Salt	1/8 tsp.	0.5 mL
Canned kernel corn, drained	1 cup	250 mL
Salsa	1/2 cup	125 mL

Pour water into medium saucepan. Bring to a boil. Add rice. Stir. Reduce heat to medium-low. Simmer, covered, for 15 minutes, without stirring. Remove from heat. Let stand, covered, for about 5 minutes until rice is tender and liquid is absorbed. Fluff with fork. Cover to keep warm.

Meanwhile, heat cooking oil in large frying pan on medium-high. Add next 4 ingredients. Cook for about 4 minutes, stirring often, until mushrooms start to brown.

Add corn and salsa. Stir. Add to rice. Stir. Makes about 4 cups (1 L).

1/2 cup (125 mL): 133 Calories; 1.6 g Total Fat (0.7 g Mono, 0.4 g Poly, 0.1 g Sat); 0 mg Cholesterol; 25 g Carbohydrate; 1 g Fibre; 3 g Protein; 180 mg Sodium

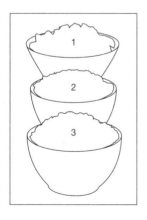

1. Chili Cheese Potatoes, page 128
2. Sweet Curried Rice, page 119
3. Tunisian Couscous, page 121

Props: Skye McGhie
        Oneida

Chili Cheese Potatoes

The heat of chili paste and the saltiness of Parmesan give depth and robust flavour to a perfectly roasted baby potato.

Cooking oil	1 tbsp.	15 mL
Chili paste (sambal oelek)	1 tsp.	5 mL
Salt	1/4 tsp.	1 mL
Baby potatoes, quartered	1 lb.	454 g
Grated Parmesan cheese	1/4 cup	60 mL

Preheat oven to 450°F (230°C). Whisk first 3 ingredients in medium bowl.

Add potato. Toss. Arrange in single layer on greased baking sheet with sides. Cook in oven for about 20 minutes, stirring occasionally, until tender and browned. Transfer to serving dish.

Sprinkle with cheese. Makes about 2 1/2 cups (625 mL).

1/2 cup (125 mL): 123 Calories; 4.6 g Total Fat (1.6 g Mono, 0.8 g Poly, 1.4 g Sat); 6 mg Cholesterol; 16 g Carbohydrate; 1 g Fibre; 5 g Protein; 245 mg Sodium

Pictured on page 126.

Tex-Mex Veggie Stir-Fry

Give your veggies a Tex-Mex kick with salsa and cheese. Serve with grilled meats or wrap up in a tortilla, burrito-style.

Cooking oil	1 tsp.	5 mL
Sliced onion	1 cup	250 mL
Thinly sliced carrot	1 cup	250 mL
Quartered fresh white mushrooms	2 cups	500 mL
Sliced red pepper	1 cup	250 mL
Salsa	1 cup	250 mL
Grated Mexican cheese blend	1/2 cup	125 mL

Heat large frying pan or wok on medium-high until very hot. Add cooking oil. Add onion and carrot. Stir-fry for 2 minutes.

(continued on next page)

Add mushrooms and red pepper. Stir-fry for about 4 minutes until carrot is tender-crisp.

Add salsa. Heat and stir for about 2 minutes until liquid is almost evaporated.

Sprinkle with cheese. Reduce heat to medium-low. Cook, covered, for about 1 minute until cheese is melted. Makes about 3 1/2 cups (875 mL).

1/2 cup (125 mL): 71 Calories; 3.4 g Total Fat (0.4 g Mono, 0.2 g Poly, 1.5 g Sat); 7 mg Cholesterol; 7 g Carbohydrate; 1 g Fibre; 3 g Protein; 200 mg Sodium

Papas Bravas

A popular tapas dish in Spain, these spicy home fries are a great accompaniment to a grilled steak or burger.

Baby potatoes, quartered	1 lb.	454 g
Olive (or cooking) oil	2 tsp.	10 mL
Salt	1/8 tsp.	0.5 mL
Pepper	1/8 tsp.	0.5 mL
Mayonnaise	1/4 cup	60 mL
Tomato sauce	1 tbsp.	15 mL
Lemon juice	2 tsp.	10 mL
Grated lemon zest (see Tip, page 48)	1/2 tsp.	2 mL
Cayenne pepper	1/4 tsp.	1 mL
Garlic powder	1/8 tsp.	0.5 mL
Salt, sprinkle		
Pepper, sprinkle		

Preheat oven to 450°F (230°C). Toss first 4 ingredients in medium bowl. Arrange in single layer on greased baking sheet with sides. Cook in oven for about 20 minutes, stirring occasionally, until tender and browned. Transfer to serving dish.

Meanwhile, combine remaining 8 ingredients in small bowl. Drizzle over potato mixture. Makes about 2 1/2 cups (625 mL).

1/2 cup (125 mL): 173 Calories; 10.7 g Total Fat (1.3 g Mono, 0.3 g Poly, 1.5 g Sat); 4 mg Cholesterol; 17 g Carbohydrate; 1 g Fibre; 2 g Protein; 141 mg Sodium

Pictured on page 18.

Pepper Cream Mashed Potatoes

Don't bother with the peeling! The skins add a rustic, gourmet element to creamy and rich mashed potatoes.

Baby potatoes, halved	2 lbs.	900 g
Ranch dressing	1/4 cup	60 mL
Cream cheese	2 tbsp.	30 mL
Salt	1/2 tsp.	2 mL
Pepper	1/2 tsp.	2 mL

Pour water into large saucepan until about 1 inch (2.5 cm) deep. Add potato. Cover. Bring to a boil. Reduce heat to medium. Boil gently for about 15 minutes until soft. Drain. Mash.

Add remaining 4 ingredients. Mash. Makes about 4 cups (1 L).

1/2 cup (125 mL): 143 Calories; 5.1 g Total Fat (0 g Mono, 0 g Poly, 1.4 g Sat); 6 mg Cholesterol; 21 g Carbohydrate; 1 g Fibre; 3 g Protein; 236 mg Sodium

Pictured on page 53.

Creamy Confetti Corn

Turn your weeknight meal into a celebration with the bright colours and comforting flavours of this creamy side dish.

Butter	1 tbsp.	15 mL
Finely chopped red pepper	1/4 cup	60 mL
All-purpose flour	2 tsp.	10 mL
Milk	1/2 cup	125 mL
Can of kernel corn, drained	12 oz.	341 mL
Sliced green onion	1/4 cup	60 mL
Cayenne pepper, just a pinch		
Salt, just a pinch		

Melt butter in medium frying pan on medium. Add red pepper. Cook for about 2 minutes, stirring often, until softened.

Add flour. Heat and stir for 1 minute. Slowly add milk, stirring constantly, until boiling and thickened.

(continued on next page)

Add remaining 4 ingredients. Stir. Cook for about 2 minutes, stirring occasionally, until corn is heated through. Makes about 1 3/4 cups (425 mL).

1/4 cup (60 mL): 62 Calories; 2.2 g Total Fat (0.5 g Mono, 0.1 g Poly, 1.1 g Sat); 5 mg Cholesterol; 7 g Carbohydrate; 1 g Fibre; 2 g Protein; 153 mg Sodium

Couscous Primavera

Named after the bright colours of spring, primavera dishes often have a bevy of mixed vegetables, and this couscous doesn't disappoint. The mild garlic, herb and Parmesan flavours make for a very versatile side dish.

Butter	1 tbsp.	15 mL
Chopped onion	1/2 cup	125 mL
Dried basil	1/4 tsp.	1 mL
Dried oregano	1/4 tsp.	1 mL
Garlic clove, minced	1	1
(or 1/4 tsp., 1 mL, powder)		
Pepper	1/8 tsp.	0.5 mL
Prepared chicken broth	1 1/2 cups	375 mL
Frozen mixed vegetables, thawed and larger pieces chopped	3/4 cup	175 mL
Couscous	1 cup	250 mL
Chopped tomato	1/2 cup	125 mL
Grated Parmesan cheese	1/4 cup	60 mL

Melt butter in medium saucepan on medium. Add next 5 ingredients. Cook, uncovered, for about 5 minutes, stirring often, until onion is softened.

Add broth. Bring to a boil.

Add vegetables. Heat and stir for 1 minute. Add couscous. Stir. Remove from heat. Let stand, covered, for 5 minutes. Fluff with fork.

Add tomato and cheese. Stir. Makes about 3 1/2 cups (875 mL).

1/2 cup (125 mL): 109 Calories; 3.5 g Total Fat (0.5 g Mono, 0.2 g Poly, 2.0 g Sat); 9 mg Cholesterol; 17 g Carbohydrate; 1 g Fibre; 5 g Protein; 409 mg Sodium

Pictured on front cover.

Hot Crumble-Topped Puddings

*Think outside the box! You've got everything you need for this pudding that's
served warm and topped with a deliciously rich crumble.*

CRUMBLE TOPPING

Medium unsweetened coconut	1/3 cup	75 mL
All-purpose flour	3 tbsp.	50 mL
Brown sugar, packed	1 tbsp.	15 mL
Cold butter	2 tbsp.	30 mL

PUDDING

Brown sugar, packed	1/4 cup	60 mL
All-purpose flour	2 tbsp.	30 mL
Cornstarch	2 tbsp.	30 mL
Salt	1/8 tsp.	0.5 mL
Large egg, fork-beaten	1	1
Milk	2 cups	500 mL
Butter	2 tsp.	10 mL
Vanilla extract	1 tsp.	5 mL

Crumble Topping: Preheat oven to 400°F (205°C). Combine first
3 ingredients in small bowl. Cut in butter until mixture resembles fine
crumbs. Transfer to ungreased 9 x 9 inch (22 x 22 cm) pan. Bake for about
8 minutes, stirring often to break up large pieces, until golden. Cool.

Pudding: Meanwhile, combine first 4 ingredients in medium saucepan.
Add egg and milk. Whisk until smooth. Cook, uncovered, on medium for
about 11 minutes, stirring constantly, until boiling and thickened. Remove
from heat.

Add butter and vanilla. Stir until butter is melted. Spoon into 4 serving
bowls. Scatter Crumble Topping over pudding. Makes 4 puddings.

*1 pudding: 295 Calories; 13.9 g Total Fat (2.6 g Mono, 0.3 g Poly, 9.4 g Sat); 81 mg Cholesterol;
36 g Carbohydrate; 1 g Fibre; 7 g Protein; 217 mg Sodium*

Quick Company Cake

Need dessert in a hurry? Make this attractive and impressive cake with ingredients on hand—in less time than it would take to go out and buy one.

All-purpose flour	1 cup	250 mL
Granulated sugar	1 cup	250 mL
Baking soda	1/2 tsp.	2 mL
Salt	1/2 tsp.	2 mL
Large eggs, fork-beaten	2	2
Sour cream	1/3 cup	75 mL
Water	1/3 cup	75 mL
Cooking oil	1/4 cup	60 mL
Vanilla extract	1 1/2 tsp.	7 mL
Semi-sweet chocolate chips	1 cup	250 mL
Sour cream	1/2 cup	125 mL

Preheat oven to 375°F (190°C). Combine first 4 ingredients in large bowl. Make a well in centre.

Add next 5 ingredients to well. Stir until just moistened. Spread evenly in greased 9 x 9 inch (22 x 22 cm) pan. Bake for about 22 minutes until wooden pick inserted in centre of cake comes out clean.

Meanwhile, combine chocolate chips and second amount of sour cream in microwave-safe bowl. Microwave, uncovered, on medium (50%) for about 90 seconds, stirring every 30 seconds, until chocolate is almost melted (see Tip, below). Stir until smooth. Spread over cake. Cuts into 16 pieces.

1 piece: 189 Calories; 9.3 g Total Fat (3.1 g Mono, 1.1 g Poly, 3.8 g Sat); 35 mg Cholesterol; 25 g Carbohydrate; 1 g Fibre; 2 g Protein; 125 mg Sodium

Pictured on page 72.

 tip The microwaves used in our test kitchen are 900 watts—but microwaves are sold in many different powers. You should be able to find the wattage of yours by opening the door and looking for the mandatory label. If your microwave is more than 900 watts, you may need to reduce the cooking time.

Peach Melba Shortcakes

If time is short, make shortcakes! Freshly made biscuits dripping with a creamy, fruity sauce are sprinkled with crunchy toasted coconut for a simply satisfying end to dinner.

Biscuit mix	1 cup	250 mL
Milk	1/4 cup	60 mL
Brown sugar, packed	2 tbsp.	30 mL
Butter	2 tbsp.	30 mL
Can of sliced peaches in juice, drained	28 oz.	796 mL
Raspberry jam	3 tbsp.	50 mL
Peach yogurt	1/4 cup	60 mL
Medium unsweetened coconut, toasted (see Tip, page 40)	2 tbsp.	30 mL

Preheat oven to 450°F (230°C). Put biscuit mix into small bowl. Make a well in centre.

Add milk to well. Stir until just moistened. Drop 4 portions of batter, using 3 tbsp. (50 mL) for each, about 2 inches (5 cm) apart onto greased baking sheet. Bake for about 9 minutes until golden and wooden pick inserted in centre of biscuit comes out clean. Transfer to cutting board. Let stand for 5 minutes. Cut in half horizontally. Place, cut-side up, on 4 serving plates.

Meanwhile, combine brown sugar and butter in large frying pan. Cook on medium-high for about 3 minutes, stirring occasionally, until butter is melted and mixture is bubbling.

Add peaches. Cook for about 4 minutes, stirring occasionally, until peaches are heated through.

Spread jam on biscuit halves. Spoon peach mixture over top. Spoon yogurt over peach mixture. Sprinkle with coconut. Makes 4 shortcakes.

1 shortcake: 421 Calories; 11.2 g Total Fat (1.6 g Mono, 0.3 g Poly, 5.9 g Sat); 17 mg Cholesterol; 79 g Carbohydrate; 5 g Fibre; 5 g Protein; 472 mg Sodium

Sachertorte Bites

Inspired by the classic Viennese torte that combines chocolate cake and apricot jam, these eggless cakes make a quick chocolate "fix."

All-purpose flour	1/2 cup	125 mL
Granulated sugar	1/3 cup	75 mL
Cocoa, sifted if lumpy	2 tbsp.	30 mL
Baking soda	1/8 tsp.	0.5 mL
Salt	1/8 tsp.	0.5 mL
Milk	1/3 cup	75 mL
Cooking oil	2 tbsp.	30 mL
White vinegar	1/2 tsp.	2 mL
Vanilla extract	1/4 tsp.	1 mL
Apricot jam	1/4 cup	60 mL
Water	1 tsp.	5 mL
Lemon juice	3/4 tsp.	4 mL
Semi-sweet chocolate chips	2 tbsp.	30 mL
Butter	1 tsp.	5 mL

Preheat oven to 375°F (190°C). Combine first 5 ingredients in medium bowl. Make a well in centre.

Combine next 4 ingredients in small bowl. Add to well. Stir until just moistened. Fill 12 greased mini-muffin cups 3/4 full. Bake for about 10 minutes until wooden pick inserted in centre of cake comes out clean. Let stand in pan for 5 minutes.

Meanwhile, combine next 3 ingredients in small microwave-safe bowl. Microwave, uncovered, on medium (50%) for about 30 seconds until melted. Stir.

Combine chocolate chips and butter in separate small microwave-safe bowl. Microwave, uncovered, on medium (50%) for about 30 seconds, stirring every 10 seconds, until chocolate is almost melted (see Tip, page 133). Stir until smooth. Split cake bites in half. Spread apricot mixture over cut sides of 12 halves. Top with remaining halves. Transfer to serving plate. Drizzle chocolate mixture over cake bites. Makes 12 cake bites.

1 cake bite: 92 Calories; 3.3 g Total Fat (1.6 g Mono, 0.7 g Poly, 0.7 g Sat); 1 mg Cholesterol; 16 g Carbohydrate; trace Fibre; 1 g Protein; 46 mg Sodium

Pictured on page 143.

Jewelled Fruit Medley

The best part of dinner is smelling dessert cooking! Try this fruity mix over ice cream or biscuits.

Water	2 cups	500 mL
Raisins	1 1/4 cups	300 mL
Dried cranberries	1 cup	250 mL
Halved dried apricots	1 cup	250 mL
Lemon juice	3 tbsp.	50 mL
Brown sugar, packed	2 tbsp.	30 mL
Grated lemon zest (see Tip, page 48)	1 tsp.	5 mL
Ground cinnamon	1/2 tsp.	2 mL
Ground ginger	1/4 tsp.	1 mL

Combine all 9 ingredients in medium saucepan. Bring to a boil. Reduce heat to medium. Boil gently, uncovered, for about 15 minutes, stirring occasionally, until apricot is softened and liquid is absorbed. Makes about 2 2/3 cups (650 mL).

1/2 cup (125 mL): 267 Calories; trace Total Fat (0 g Mono, trace Poly, 0 g Sat); 0 mg Cholesterol; 68 g Carbohydrate; 5 g Fibre; 2 g Protein; 28 mg Sodium

Apricot Coconut Mini-Cakes

The icing on the cake is a cinnamon sugar sprinkle. Sweet little treats in no time!

Large egg	1	1
Apricot jam	1/3 cup	75 mL
Chopped dried apricot	1/3 cup	75 mL
Medium unsweetened coconut	1/4 cup	60 mL
Butter, melted	3 tbsp.	50 mL
Milk	2 tbsp.	30 mL
Vanilla extract	3/4 tsp.	4 mL
All-purpose flour	1/2 cup	125 mL
Baking powder	1/2 tsp.	2 mL
Salt	1/8 tsp.	0.5 mL
Granulated sugar	2 tsp.	10 mL
Ground cinnamon	1/8 tsp.	0.5 mL

(continued on next page)

Desserts

Preheat oven to 375°F (190°C). Whisk first 7 ingredients in medium bowl until combined.

Combine next 3 ingredients in small bowl. Add to egg mixture. Stir until no dry flour remains. Spoon into 4 greased 6 oz. (170 mL) ramekins.

Combine sugar and cinnamon in small cup. Sprinkle over batter. Bake for about 18 minutes until wooden pick inserted in centre of cake comes out clean. Makes 4 cakes.

1 cake: 281 Calories; 12.8 g Total Fat (2.4 g Mono, 0.4 g Poly, 8.5 g Sat); 77 mg Cholesterol; 40 g Carbohydrate; 2 g Fibre; 4 g Protein; 242 mg Sodium

Cranberry Coconut Brownies

Sweet, chocolatey flavour pairs well with tangy cranberries. These will freeze well, but we doubt you'll have any leftovers because they taste like 'more!'

All-purpose flour	1/2 cup	125 mL
Cocoa, sifted if lumpy	1/2 cup	125 mL
Medium unsweetened coconut	1/2 cup	125 mL
Salt	1/4 tsp.	1 mL
Large eggs	2	2
Granulated sugar	1 cup	250 mL
Butter, melted	1/3 cup	75 mL
Sour cream	1/3 cup	75 mL
Dried cranberries	1/2 cup	125 mL

Preheat oven to 350°F (175°C). Combine first 4 ingredients in small bowl.

Whisk next 4 ingredients in medium bowl until combined. Add flour mixture. Stir well.

Add cranberries. Stir. Fill 24 greased mini-muffin cups full. Bake for about 15 minutes until wooden pick inserted in centre of brownie comes out moist but not wet with batter. Do not overbake. Let stand in pan for 5 minutes. Makes 24 brownies.

1 brownie: 100 Calories; 4.6 g Total Fat (0.7 g Mono, 0.1 g Poly, 3.0 g Sat); 27 mg Cholesterol; 14 g Carbohydrate; 1 g Fibre; 1 g Protein; 49 mg Sodium

Pictured on page 90 and on back cover.

Raisin Rice Pudding

Warm cinnamon flavours fill a creamy rice pudding. Tangy yogurt makes a lovely finishing touch.

Water	2 1/2 cups	625 mL
Long-grain white rice, rinsed and drained	1 cup	250 mL
Raisins	1/2 cup	125 mL
Plain yogurt	1 cup	250 mL
Granulated sugar	1/3 cup	75 mL
Milk	1/4 cup	60 mL
Vanilla extract	1 tsp.	5 mL
Ground cinnamon	1/4 tsp.	1 mL

Combine first 3 ingredients in medium saucepan. Bring to a boil. Reduce heat to medium-low. Simmer, covered, for 15 minutes, without stirring. Remove from heat. Let stand, covered, for about 5 minutes until rice is tender and liquid is absorbed. Fluff with fork.

Meanwhile, stir remaining 5 ingredients in large bowl until sugar is dissolved. Add rice mixture. Stir. Makes about 5 cups (1.25 L).

1 cup (250 mL): 290 Calories; 1.1 g Total Fat (0.2 g Mono, 0.1 g Poly, 0.7 g Sat); 5 mg Cholesterol; 62 g Carbohydrate; 1 g Fibre; 6 g Protein; 46 mg Sodium

Double-Chocolate Puddings

Chocolate and almonds make natural partners, but you could substitute sliced banana for a crunch-free alternative to this eggless pudding.

Granulated sugar	1/3 cup	75 mL
Cocoa, sifted if lumpy	1/4 cup	60 mL
Cornstarch	3 tbsp.	50 mL
Salt, just a pinch		
Milk	2 cups	500 mL
Butter	1 tsp.	5 mL
Vanilla extract	1 tsp.	5 mL
Semi-sweet chocolate chips	1/4 cup	60 mL
Sliced almonds, toasted (see Tip, page 40)	1/4 cup	60 mL

(continued on next page)

138 Desserts

Combine first 4 ingredients in medium saucepan. Add milk. Whisk until smooth. Cook, uncovered, on medium for about 6 minutes, stirring frequently, until boiling and thickened. Remove from heat.

Add butter and vanilla. Stir until butter is melted. Spoon into 4 serving bowls.

Scatter chocolate chips and almonds over top. Makes 4 puddings.

1 pudding: 263 Calories; 9.3 g Total Fat (4.0 g Mono, 1.0 g Poly, 3.5 g Sat); 10 mg Cholesterol; 40 g Carbohydrate; 2 g Fibre; 7 g Protein; 74 mg Sodium

Pictured on page 143.

Mango Berry Crisp

Fruit crisp with a mango twist! The sweet-tart fruit flavours and crunchy buttery topping are best served warm.

Frozen mango pieces, thawed	3 cups	750 mL
Frozen mixed berries, thawed	2 cups	500 mL
Brown sugar, packed	2 tbsp.	30 mL
All-purpose flour	1 tbsp.	15 mL
Grated lemon zest	1/4 tsp.	1 mL
Butter	1/3 cup	75 mL
Quick-cooking rolled oats	1 cup	250 mL
Brown sugar, packed	1/3 cup	75 mL
All-purpose flour	1/4 cup	60 mL
Vanilla extract	1/4 tsp.	1 mL
Salt, sprinkle		

Preheat oven to 425°F (220°C). Combine first 5 ingredients in medium bowl. Transfer to greased 8 x 8 inch (20 x 20 cm) microwave-safe baking dish. Microwave, uncovered, on high (100%) for about 5 minutes until hot. Stir.

Meanwhile, melt butter in small saucepan on medium. Add remaining 5 ingredients. Stir until mixture resembles coarse crumbs. Scatter over mango mixture. Bake for about 15 minutes until top is golden and fruit is bubbling. Serves 6.

1 serving: 307 Calories; 11.3 g Total Fat (2.7 g Mono, 0.4 g Poly, 6.4 g Sat); 27 mg Cholesterol; 50 g Carbohydrate; 4 g Fibre; 4 g Protein; 80 mg Sodium

Pictured on page 53.

Cranberry Pear Cobbler

Make a Sunday dinner-worthy dessert any day of the week. This pear cobbler is accented with just the right amount of ginger heat and cranberry tartness.

Cans of pear halves in juice (14 oz., 398 mL, each), drained and juice reserved, chopped	2	2
Dried cranberries	3/4 cup	175 mL
Brown sugar, packed	2 tbsp.	30 mL
Ground ginger	1/2 tsp.	2 mL
Reserved pear juice	1 cup	250 mL
Cornstarch	1 tbsp.	15 mL
Biscuit mix	1 cup	250 mL
Reserved pear juice	1/3 cup	75 mL
Ground ginger	1/4 tsp.	1 mL
Brown sugar, packed	1 tbsp.	15 mL

Preheat oven to 400°F (205°C). Combine first 4 ingredients in ungreased 8 x 8 inch (20 x 20 cm) baking dish.

Whisk first amount of pear juice into cornstarch in small cup until smooth. Drizzle over pear mixture. Stir well. Microwave, uncovered, on high (100%) for 5 to 6 minutes, stirring once, until heated through.

Meanwhile, stir next 3 ingredients in small bowl until just moistened. Drop batter onto pear mixture, using about 1 tbsp. (15 mL) for each.

Sprinkle second amount of brown sugar over batter. Bake for about 15 minutes until biscuits are golden and wooden pick inserted in centre of biscuit comes out clean. Serves 6.

1 serving: 222 Calories; 2.5 g Total Fat (trace Mono, trace Poly, 0.6 g Sat); 0 mg Cholesterol; 50 g Carbohydrate; 3 g Fibre; 2 g Protein; 277 mg Sodium

Pictured on page 143.

Welsh Rarebit

There's often talk of rabbits when the topic of Welsh Rarebit (also called Welsh Rabbit) comes up, but it's really just cheese on toast (the Welsh way).

Butter	2 tbsp.	30 mL
Small garlic clove, minced (or 1/8 tsp., 0.5 mL, powder)	1	1
All-purpose flour	1 tbsp.	15 mL
Milk	1/2 cup	125 mL
Dijon mustard	1 tsp.	5 mL
Worcestershire sauce	1/4 tsp.	1 mL
Cayenne pepper	1/8 tsp.	0.5 mL
Salt	1/8 tsp.	0.5 mL
Pepper	1/4 tsp.	1 mL
Grated Cheddar cheese	2 cups	500 mL
Whole-wheat bread slices, toasted	4	4

Melt butter in medium saucepan on medium. Add garlic. Heat and stir for about 1 minute until garlic is fragrant.

Add flour. Heat and stir for 1 minute. Slowly add milk, stirring constantly until boiling and thickened.

Add next 5 ingredients. Stir.

Add cheese. Heat and stir for about 2 minutes until cheese is melted.

Spoon over toast slices. Serve immediately. Makes 4 Welsh rarebits.

1 Welsh rarebit: 369 Calories; 25.9 g Total Fat (7.4 g Mono, 1.0 g Poly, 16.0 g Sat); 76 mg Cholesterol; 17 g Carbohydrate; 2 g Fibre; 18 g Protein; 648 mg Sodium

Paré Pointer

A king's round table suffered from insomnia because of all the sleepless knights.

Pantry Explorer Trail Mix

Less time in the kitchen means more time to play. Toasted almonds,
sunflower seeds and cinnamon make great additions to a standard trail mix.

Brown sugar, packed	2 tbsp.	30 mL
Butter	2 tbsp.	30 mL
Ground cinnamon	1/2 tsp.	2 mL
Granola	2 cups	500 mL
Chopped dried apricot	1/2 cup	125 mL
Dried cranberries	1/2 cup	125 mL
Raisins	1/2 cup	125 mL
Semi-sweet chocolate chips	1/2 cup	125 mL

Put first 3 ingredients into large frying pan. Cook on medium for about 3 minutes, stirring occasionally, until butter is melted.

Add next 4 ingredients. Heat and stir for about 2 minutes until coated. Spread in 9 x 13 inch (22 x 33 cm) pan. Chill for about 18 minutes until cool. Transfer to medium bowl.

Add chocolate chips. Stir. Makes about 4 1/2 cups (1.1 L).

1 cup (250 mL): 209 Calories; 7.6 g Total Fat (1.6 g Mono, 0.2 g Poly, 3.3 g Sat); 7 mg Cholesterol; 35 g Carbohydrate; 3 g Fibre; 3 g Protein; 36 mg Sodium

Pictured on page 144.

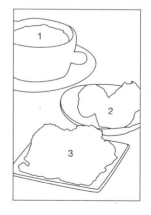

1. Double-Chocolate Puddings, page 138
2. Sachertorte Bites, page 135
3. Cranberry Pear Cobbler, page 140

Props: H & H (House and Home)
abbott

PBJ Minis

*The classic combination of peanut butter and jam in a mini-muffin—the
perfect easy-to-grab snack for all ages.*

All-purpose flour	1 cup	250 mL
Quick-cooking rolled oats	3/4 cup	175 mL
Baking powder	1 1/2 tsp.	7 mL
Baking soda	1 tsp.	5 mL
Salt	1/2 tsp.	2 mL
Brown sugar, packed	2/3 cup	150 mL
Smooth peanut butter	1/2 cup	125 mL
Large eggs	2	2
Milk	1/2 cup	125 mL
Cooking oil	2 tbsp.	30 mL
Vanilla extract	2 tsp.	10 mL
Raspberry jam	2 tbsp.	30 mL

Preheat oven to 400°F (205°C). Combine first 5 ingredients in large bowl.
Make a well in centre.

Beat brown sugar and peanut butter in medium bowl until combined. Add
eggs, 1 at a time, beating well after each addition.

Add next 3 ingredients. Stir. Add to well. Stir until just moistened. Fill
24 greased mini-muffin cups 3/4 full.

Spoon 1/4 tsp. (1 mL) jam onto centre of each mini-muffin. Bake for about
10 minutes until wooden pick inserted in centre of mini-muffin comes out
clean. Let stand in pan for 5 minutes before removing to wire rack to cool.
Makes 24 mini-muffins.

*1 mini-muffin: 106 Calories; 4.6 g Total Fat (0.7 g Mono,
0.3 g Poly, 0.8 g Sat); 18 mg Cholesterol; 14 g Carbohydrate;
1 g Fibre; 3 g Protein; 171 mg Sodium*

Pictured at left.

1. PBJ Minis, above
2. Roasted Red Pepper Dip, page 147
3. Pantry Explorer Trail Mix, page 142

BLT Cukes

Enjoy the flavours of a bacon, lettuce and tomato sandwich tucked into a thick slice of cucumber. A refreshing summertime snack!

Finely chopped romaine lettuce mix, lightly packed	1/2 cup	125 mL
Finely chopped seeded tomato	1/4 cup	60 mL
Mayonnaise	2 tbsp.	30 mL
Bacon slices, cooked crisp and crumbled	2	2
Salt	1/8 tsp.	0.5 mL
Pepper	1/8 tsp.	0.5 mL
English cucumber slices (with peel), about 3/4 inch (2 cm) thick	16	16

Combine first 6 ingredients in small bowl.

Scoop out centres of cucumber slices with melon baller, leaving 1/4 inch (6 mm) border. Fill with lettuce mixture. Makes 16 cucumber rounds.

1 cucumber round: 20 Calories; 1.7 g Total Fat (0.2 g Mono, trace Poly, 0.3 g Sat); 2 mg Cholesterol; 1 g Carbohydrate; trace Fibre; 1 g Protein; 46 mg Sodium

Corn Fritter Bites

Mini corn muffins with a little chili heat are perfect for a southwestern-style meal. Use them to accompany your favourite chili or for a late-afternoon snack. Use the leftover corn in Corn and Black Bean Salsa, page 150, or toss it into salads, soups or stews.

All-purpose flour	1 cup	250 mL
Baking powder	1 tsp.	5 mL
Chili powder	1/2 tsp.	2 mL
Salt	1/2 tsp.	2 mL
Cayenne pepper	1/8 tsp.	0.5 mL

(continued on next page)

Large egg, fork-beaten	1	1
Sour cream	3/4 cup	175 mL
Canned kernel corn, drained	1/2 cup	125 mL
Water	1/4 cup	60 mL
Roasted red peppers, chopped	2 tbsp.	30 mL
Sliced green onion	2 tbsp.	30 mL

Preheat oven to 400°F (205°C). Combine first 5 ingredients in medium bowl. Make a well in centre.

Add remaining 6 ingredients to well. Stir until just moistened. Fill 24 greased mini-muffin cups 3/4 full. Bake for about 14 minutes until wooden pick inserted in centre of fritter comes out clean. Let stand in pan for 5 minutes before removing to wire rack to cool. Makes 24 fritters.

1 fritter: 40 Calories; 1.5 g Total Fat (0 g Mono, 0 g Poly, 0.9 g Sat); 14 mg Cholesterol;
5 g Carbohydrate; trace Fibre; 1 g Protein; 103 mg Sodium

Roasted Red Pepper Dip

The smoky flavours of roasted red pepper and feta shine in this dip that's
hearty like hummus. Try it with raw vegetables or toast points.

Can of chickpeas (garbanzo beans), rinsed and drained	19 oz.	540 mL
Jar of roasted red peppers, drained, coarsely chopped	12 oz.	340 mL
Crumbled feta cheese	3/4 cup	175 mL
Mayonnaise	1/2 cup	125 mL
Lemon juice	2 tbsp.	30 mL
Dried crushed chilies	1/4 tsp.	1 mL
Garlic powder	1/4 tsp.	1 mL
Salt	1/2 tsp.	2 mL
Pepper	1/4 tsp.	1 mL

Process all 9 ingredients in food processor, scraping down sides if necessary, until smooth. Makes about 2 3/4 cups (675 mL).

1/2 cup (125 mL): 362 Calories; 21.9 g Total Fat (1.3 g Mono, 0.9 g Poly, 5.2 g Sat);
25 mg Cholesterol; 26 g Carbohydrate; 4 g Fibre; 10 g Protein; 1273 mg Sodium

Pictured on page 144.

Spice Cookies

When nothing but a cookie will do, why not try these quick-to-bake, spicy treats?

Large egg, fork-beaten	1	1
All-purpose flour	2/3 cup	150 mL
Brown sugar, packed	1/3 cup	75 mL
Cooking oil	2 tbsp.	30 mL
Vanilla extract	1/2 tsp.	2 mL
Baking powder	1/4 tsp.	1 mL
Baking soda	1/4 tsp.	1 mL
Ground allspice	1/4 tsp.	1 mL
Ground cinnamon	1/4 tsp.	1 mL
Salt	1/4 tsp.	1 mL

Preheat oven to 350°F (175°C). Stir all 10 ingredients in medium bowl until just moistened. Drop, using 1 tbsp. (15 mL) for each, about 1 inch (2.5 cm) apart onto greased cookie sheet. Bake for about 10 minutes until edges are golden. Let stand on cookie sheet for 5 minutes before removing to wire rack to cool. Makes about 10 cookies.

1 cookie: 87 Calories; 3.3 g Total Fat (1.6 g Mono, 0.8 g Poly, 0.4 g Sat); 22 mg Cholesterol; 13 g Carbohydrate; trace Fibre; 1 g Protein; 113 mg Sodium

Paré Pointer
The cat disappeared so fast that the dog went barking up the wrong tree.

Maple Granola Bars

Tired of the same old bars? These oat bars have a delightful vanilla and maple aroma and a delicate crispness. Wrap any leftovers and store them at room temperature for up to one week.

Butter	2/3 cup	150 mL
Maple syrup	1/2 cup	125 mL
Brown sugar, packed	1/3 cup	75 mL
Vanilla extract	1 tsp.	5 mL
Quick-cooking rolled oats	3 cups	750 mL
All-purpose flour	1 cup	250 mL

Preheat oven to 350°F (175°C). Combine first 4 ingredients in large saucepan. Heat and stir on medium for about 4 minutes until butter is melted.

Add oats and flour. Stir well. Press into greased 9 x 13 inch (22 x 33 cm) pan. Score into 24 bars with sharp knife. Bake for about 22 minutes until golden. Cut along scoring. Makes 24 granola bars.

1 granola bar: 132 Calories; 5.8 g Total Fat (1.3 g Mono, 0.2 g Poly, 3.2 g Sat); 13 mg Cholesterol; 18 g Carbohydrate; 1 g Fibre; 2 g Protein; 38 mg Sodium

Chocolate Crunch Clusters

These rich tasting, nô-bake cookies are fun for kids of all ages!

Semi-sweet chocolate chips	2 cups	500 mL
Butter	1/4 cup	60 mL
Smooth peanut butter	1/4 cup	60 mL
Granola	2 cups	500 mL
Chopped dried apricot	1 cup	250 mL

Heat first 3 ingredients in large heavy saucepan on lowest heat, stirring often, until chocolate is almost melted. Remove from heat. Stir until smooth.

Add granola and apricot. Stir until coated. Drop, using 1 tbsp. (15 mL) for each, onto waxed paper-lined cookie sheets. Chill for about 10 minutes until set. Makes about 44 cookies.

1 cookie: 75 Calories; 4.6 g Total Fat (1.0 g Mono, 0.1 g Poly, 2.2 g Sat); 3 mg Cholesterol; 9 g Carbohydrate; 1 g Fibre; 1 g Protein; 19 mg Sodium

Lime Cucumber Lassi

An Indian beverage, lassi comes in sweet or savoury varieties. The refreshing coolness of yogurt, lime and cucumber makes this savoury version a must-try for a hot day.

Chopped peeled English cucumber, seeds removed	1 1/2 cups	375 mL
Plain yogurt	1 cup	250 mL
Sour cream	1 cup	250 mL
Crushed ice	1/2 cup	125 mL
Milk	1/2 cup	125 mL
Liquid honey	2 tsp.	10 mL
Lime juice	1 tsp.	5 mL
Grated lime zest (see Tip, page 48)	1/4 tsp.	1 mL
Ground cumin	1/4 tsp.	1 mL
Ground ginger	1/4 tsp.	1 mL
Salt, just a pinch		
English cucumber slices (with peel), for garnish		

Process first 11 ingredients in blender or food processor until smooth. Pour into 4 glasses.

Garnish with cucumber slices. Makes about 4 1/2 cups (1.1 L).

1 cup (250 mL): 169 Calories; 10.0 g Total Fat (0.1 g Mono, trace Poly, 7 g Sat); 42 mg Cholesterol; 10 g Carbohydrate; trace Fibre; 6 g Protein; 71 mg Sodium

Corn and Black Bean Salsa

So easy to make, so easy to eat. Impress your guests with this flavourful dip. Refrigerate the leftover black beans and corn for later use in a salad or stew.

Canned kernel corn, drained	1/2 cup	125 mL
Salsa	1/3 cup	75 mL
Canned black beans, rinsed and drained	1/4 cup	60 mL
Ketchup	2 tsp.	10 mL

Combine all 4 ingredients in small bowl. Makes about 3/4 cup (175 mL).

1/4 cup (60 mL): 63 Calories; 0.5 g Total Fat (0 g Mono, 0.2 g Poly, 0 g Sat); 0 mg Cholesterol; 11 g Carbohydrate; 2 g Fibre; 2 g Protein; 307 mg Sodium

Measurement Tables

Throughout this book measurements are given in Conventional and Metric measure. To compensate for differences between the two measurements due to rounding, a full metric measure is not always used. The cup used is the standard 8 fluid ounce. Temperature is given in degrees Fahrenheit and Celsius. Baking pan measurements are in inches and centimetres as well as quarts and litres. An exact metric conversion is given below as well as the working equivalent (Metric Standard Measure).

Spoons

Conventional Measure	Metric Exact Conversion Millilitre (mL)	Metric Standard Measure Millilitre (mL)
1/8 teaspoon (tsp.)	0.6 mL	0.5 mL
1/4 teaspoon (tsp.)	1.2 mL	1 mL
1/2 teaspoon (tsp.)	2.4 mL	2 mL
1 teaspoon (tsp.)	4.7 mL	5 mL
2 teaspoons (tsp.)	9.4 mL	10 mL
1 tablespoon (tbsp.)	14.2 mL	15 mL

Cups

Conventional Measure	Metric Exact Conversion Millilitre (mL)	Metric Standard Measure Millilitre (mL)
1/4 cup (4 tbsp.)	56.8 mL	60 mL
1/3 cup (5 1/3 tbsp.)	75.6 mL	75 mL
1/2 cup (8 tbsp.)	113.7 mL	125 mL
2/3 cup (10 2/3 tbsp.)	151.2 mL	150 mL
3/4 cup (12 tbsp.)	170.5 mL	175 mL
1 cup (16 tbsp.)	227.3 mL	250 mL
4 1/2 cups	1022.9 mL	1000 mL (1 L)

Dry Measurements

Conventional Measure Ounces (oz.)	Metric Exact Conversion Grams (g)	Metric Standard Measure Grams (g)
1 oz.	28.3 g	28 g
2 oz.	56.7 g	57 g
3 oz.	85.0 g	85 g
4 oz.	113.4 g	125 g
5 oz.	141.7 g	140 g
6 oz.	170.1 g	170 g
7 oz.	198.4 g	200 g
8 oz.	226.8 g	250 g
16 oz.	453.6 g	500 g
32 oz.	907.2 g	1000 g (1 kg)

Oven Temperatures

Fahrenheit (°F)	Celsius (°C)
175°	80°
200°	95°
225°	110°
250°	120°
275°	140°
300°	150°
325°	160°
350°	175°
375°	190°
400°	205°
425°	220°
450°	230°
475°	240°
500°	260°

Pans

Conventional Inches	Metric Centimetres
8x8 inch	20x20 cm
9x9 inch	23x23 cm
9x13 inch	23x33 cm
10x15 inch	25x38 cm
11x17 inch	28x43 cm
8x2 inch round	20x5 cm
9x2 inch round	23x5 cm
10x4 1/2 inch tube	25x11 cm
8x4x3 inch loaf	20x10x7.5 cm
9x5x3 inch loaf	23x12.5x7.5 cm

Casseroles

CANADA & BRITAIN Standard Size Casserole	Exact Metric Measure	UNITED STATES Standard Size Casserole	Exact Metric Measure
1 qt. (5 cups)	1.13 L	1 qt. (4 cups)	900 mL
1 1/2 qts. (7 1/2 cups)	1.69 L	1 1/2 qts. (6 cups)	1.35 L
2 qts. (10 cups)	2.25 L	2 qts. (8 cups)	1.8 L
2 1/2 qts. (12 1/2 cups)	2.81 L	2 1/2 qts. (10 cups)	2.25 L
3 qts. (15 cups)	3.38 L	3 qts. (12 cups)	2.7 L
4 qts. (20 cups)	4.5 L	4 qts. (16 cups)	3.6 L
5 qts. (25 cups)	5.63 L	5 qts. (20 cups)	4.5 L

Recipe Index

152

153

154

155

⌠Try it

a sample recipe from *Asian Cooking*

Minty Pawpaw Salad
Asian Cooking, Page 116

DRESSING

Lemon (or lime) juice	2 tbsp.	30 mL
Garlic clove, minced (or 1/4 tsp., 1 mL, powder)	1	1
Finely grated gingerroot, (or 1/8 tsp. 0.5 mL, ground ginger)	1/2 tsp.	2 mL
Fish sauce	2 tbsp.	30 mL
Golden corn (or cane) syrup	1 tbsp.	15 mL
Chili sauce	1 tbsp.	15 mL
Dried crushed chilies	1/8 tsp.	0.5 mL
Ripe large papayas, peeled, seeded and diced	2	2
Small red onion, cut into paper-thin slices	1	1
Small red pepper, slivered	1	1
Fresh mint leaves, chopped	1/3 cup	75 mL
Butter lettuce leaves	12 - 20	12 - 20

Dressing: Combine first 7 ingredients in small dish. Let stand at room temperature for 30 minutes to blend flavours. Makes 1/3 cup (75 mL) dressing.

Place papaya, onion, red pepper, mint and dressing in large bowl. Toss gently until well coated. Makes 4 cups (1 L) salad.

Line small bowls with 3 to 5 lettuce leaves each. Add 1 cup (250 mL) salad to each. Serves 4.

1 serving: 104 Calories; 0.4 g Total Fat; 539 mg Sodium; 3 g Protein; 25 g Carbohydrate; 4 g Dietary Fibre

If you like what we've done with **cooking**, you'll **love** what we do with **crafts**!

Complete your Original Series Collection!

- ❏ 150 Delicious Squares
- ❏ Appetizers
- ❏ Cookies
- ❏ Barbecues
- ❏ Preserves
- ❏ Slow Cooker Recipes
- ❏ Stir-Fry
- ❏ Stews, Chilies & Chowders
- ❏ Fondues
- ❏ The Rookie Cook
- ❏ Sweet Cravings
- ❏ Year-Round Grilling
- ❏ Garden Greens
- ❏ Chinese Cooking
- ❏ The Beverage Book
- ❏ Slow Cooker Dinners
- ❏ 30-Minute Weekday Meals
- ❏ Potluck Dishes
- ❏ Ground Beef Recipes
- ❏ 4-Ingredient Recipes
- ❏ Kids' Healthy Cooking
- ❏ Mostly Muffins
- ❏ Soups
- ❏ Simple Suppers
- ❏ Diabetic Cooking
- ❏ Chicken Now
- ❏ Kids Do Snacks
- ❏ Low-Fat Express
- ❏ Choosing Sides
- ❏ Perfect Pasta & Sauces
- ❏ 30-Minute Diabetic Cooking
- ❏ Healthy In A Hurry
- ❏ Table For Two
- ❏ Catch Of The Day
- ❏ Kids Do Baking
- ❏ 5-Ingredient Slow Cooker Recipes
- ❏ Diabetic Dinners
- ❏ Easy Healthy Recipes
- ❏ 30-Minute Pantry
- ❏ Everyday Barbecuing
- ❏ Meal Salads
- ❏ Healthy Slow Cooker
- ❏ Breads
- ❏ Anytime Casseroles
- ❏ Asian Cooking
  NEW *April 1/11*

Company's Coming
News Bite
Sign up

FREE Online NEWSLETTER

Subscribe to our **free** News Bite newsletter and get the following benefits:

- **Special** offers & promotions
- **FREE** recipes & cooking tips
- **Previews** of new and upcoming titles
- **Automatic** entry to exciting contests
- **Ability** to purchase new titles before they reach store shelves

Subscribe today!

www.companyscoming.com
visit our ↖ website

Each Focus Series book is a mini feature event—priced to make collecting them all especially easy.

Focus Series

- ❏ Apple Appeal
- ❏ Berries & Cream
- ❏ Carrot Craze
- ❏ Chicken Breast Finesse
- ❏ Chilled Thrills
- ❏ Chocolate Squared
- ❏ Coffee Cake Classics
- ❏ Cookie Jar Classics
- ❏ Cranberrys Cravings
- ❏ Dip, Dunk & Dab
- ❏ Easy Roasting
- ❏ Fab Finger Food
- ❏ Fruit Squared
- ❏ Hearty Soups
- ❏ Hot Bites
- ❏ Lemon Lime Zingers
- ❏ Mushroom Magic
- ❏ Salads To Go
- ❏ Shrimp Delicious
- ❏ Simmering Stews
- ❏ Simply Vegetarian
- ❏ Sips
- ❏ Skewered
- ❏ So Strawberry
- ❏ Splendid Spuds
- ❏ Steak Sizzle
- ❏ Sweet Dreams
- ❏ That's A Wrap
- ❏ Tomato Temptations
- ❏ Tossed
- ❏ Warm Desserts
- ❏ Zucchini Zone